WE ARE ONE

Lorelle Taylor

Peace Angel
Publishing

Copyright © 2020 by Lorelle Taylor
Published by Peace Angel Publishing.

All rights reserved. No part of this book may be reproduced by any mechanical, photographic, or electronic process, or in the form of a phonographic recording, nor may it be stored in a retrieval system, transmitted, or otherwise be copied for public or private use—other than for "fair use" as brief quotations embodied in articles and reviews—without prior written permission of the publisher.

ISBN 978-0-6484786-3-8 Print
ISBN 978-0-6484786-4-5 epub
ISBN 978-0-6484786-5-2 mobi

Contents

Preface ix

Introduction 1

The Word of God 3

Tomorrow's God 7
    The Future of Education 7
    The Future of Business and the Economy 8
    Consider the Consequences 10
    Be Completely Honest 15
    God is Life 16
    There's Enough 16
    Who Feels the Love? 18
    Evolution 19
    Knowing Tomorrow's God 20
    God is Everything 21
    New Spirituality Study Group 22
    Meditation, Eating, Exercising 23
    Most Important Message 24
    Love One Another as Yourself 24
    Faith in Life 25
    Dishonesty is Ingrained 26
    Time to Wake Up 28

Life in the New Spirituality 31
    Snowball of Love 31

Life in the New Spirituality 32
Communication in the New Spirituality 33
Where is the Dividing Line? 40
Communicating With Other Realms 42
Communicating With Animals 44
Seeing into Other Realms 46
Starting the Snowball of Love Rolling 49
Living In Harmony 53
Miraculous Healings 58
Resolving Differences 59
Employment 61
Stewardship 63
Gratitude 66
Highly Evolved Beings 67
Love 70
Healing 72
Who is God? 73
Look for the Blessings 74
Sex 76
Birth Control 81
How Many Partners? 82
A Balanced View of Sex 83
Love is the Answer 84

Islam 86
The Koran 86
Reconciliation 89
Democracy 92
Hell 95
Consequences 97
Idolatry 98
Sacred rites 100
Worship of God 101
Prayer 101

Cleanliness	102
Submission	103
God's Will	104
Covering Up	106
Spouses	108
Chastity	109
Punishment	110
More on Chastity	112
Lewdness	113
More Punishment	113
Homosexuality	115
Multiple Wives	116
Marriage to Non-Believers	117
Domination of Women	119
War	122
Acts of Terror	124
More Killing	125
Animal Welfare	126
Gratitude	128
We Are One	129
Punishing Schismatics	130
Controlling Others	131
Judgment Day	132
Death	135
The Term of Life	136
Creative Ability	136
God Is In All Things	136
The Light of God	137
Psychic Abilities	138
The True Faith	139
Truth in the Koran	141
Ever Changing God	142
God of Love	143

- Talking to God 144
- The Last Prophet 146
- Children of God 147
- Jews and Christians 149
- Enjoy Life 151
- Waking Up 151
- The Heart 152
- Drinking and Gambling 153
- Usury 154
- Peace 155
- Jesus' Birth and Death 156
- Protection from Devils 163
- Guardian Angels 164
- Crazy? 165
- Tafsir 165
- God's Children 166
- Everything is God 166
- Human and Animal Art 167
- Don't Muslim Practices Work? 168
- Muslim Women 169
- Circumcision 172
- Straight Path to God 174
- The Hadith 174
- God's Message 176

The Satanic Verses 178

Judaism 183

Christianity 189
- Jesus' Example 189
- Distortions 192
- The Messiah 197
- Who Killed Jesus? 199

Buddhism 203
   Karma 203
   Reincarnation 206
   Under the Bodhi Tree 208

Moving Forward 211

Insanity or Ego 218
   Submitting to Yesterday's God 222
   The Ego and Creation 225
   Life on Earth 230
   Follow Your Bliss 239
   Talking to the Prophets 241
   Saving the World 249
   What's in a Name? 253

Afterword 256

More Information 259

Acknowledgments 261

Recommended Reading 263

Bibliography 265

Preface

Although this book can be read as a stand-alone book, there are concepts in this book which may be more easily understood after first reading the book, *Getting Used to Weird: A Very Different Sort of Love Story*.[1]

You may be shocked by some parts of this book, but after you have recovered, I urge you to continue reading. You may find it is worth it.

Introduction

Angela breathed a sigh of relief. Perhaps she wasn't crazy after all. Perhaps everything that had happened to her in the last few weeks really was meant to happen. Perhaps it was all supposed to allow her to become the person who could help the world move towards the New Spirituality, the wonderful new world that the voice in her head had promised her, that God had promised her. Maybe it really was all part of God's divine plan.

She still had doubts. She still could be one step away from the psychiatric hospital, but she now also had hope. She hoped that, one day, all the world would come to know that We Are One, and that God created each and every one of us in his/her likeness—not a physical likeness—but the likeness of God's love. She could once again believe that God is love, and if God created all of the universe, then everyone and everything must be love also.

If Angela could tell her story to the world, it wouldn't matter if people didn't believe her. It wouldn't matter if they thought she was crazy. She hoped she could believe what God had told her:

"Angela, the world is ready for your book. You know this

is a work of fiction, and everyone will know they can believe it or not if they so choose, but everyone will know it is the truth. Everyone will know that you did speak to God, converse with God, receive revelations from God.

"I know you are thinking: 'What about those people who will find it too confronting?' You wonder if they will be able to cope with the revelations I have given you, if they accepted them as truth. Those people, Angela, will be able to discount it as pure fiction. Those people will understand that it is merely the workings of a crazy mind in a crazy fictional book. Everyone else will know that everything you have put into this book is true."

So, she would be crazy if that was what was required, but she would hope, just as those who heard her story would; hope that every word was true, and that love would one day rule the world.

The Word of God

"In the beginning was the Word, and the Word was with God, and the Word was God."
John 1:1 [2]

"In him was life, and the life was the light of men. The light shines in the darkness, and the darkness has not overcome it."
John 1:4-5

Angela knew she too had come into the world to shine her light in the darkness. She had come to be a confident, faithful, invincible beacon of God's love. She knew this was the role every person on the Earth could choose, if they wished—to be God's beacon, to shine light in the darkness. She knew this had also been Jesus' role, and she remembered the cover of the book she read: *I Am with You Always: True Stories of Encounters with Jesus* by G. Scott Sparrow, Ed.D.[3] The cover showed Jesus holding a lantern, a symbol of the light he brought to all those he helped; not only those in the book, but those throughout history who used his life as an example. Jesus came to speak to Angela, just as he had come to speak to many of those whose stories were related in the book. Angela knew that, just as Jesus was filled with the word and the light of God, so too could she and the rest of humanity be, if they based everything they did on love as he had.

It took her quite a few years and many lessons to arrive at this understanding. The lessons themselves were not difficult, but her attempts to apply them were. She learned a lot of her lessons from books like *The Power of Now*[4] by Eckhart Tolle, which taught her how to live in the moment, that she could control her thoughts, and to acknowledge her observing self. She learned about the law of attraction from Abraham, and Jerry and Esther Hicks, in books like *The Law of Attraction*[5] and *The Vortex*[6].

Angela learned that she could communicate with angels from Alma Daniel, Timothy Wyllie and Andrew Ramer in *Ask Your Angels*[7]. After practising the exercises in that book, she employed the same techniques in communicating with her spirit guides, deceased loved ones, and Jesus. Jesus helped her with healing and her lessons. He taught her how to raise her vibration and gave her detailed exercises to improve her skills at hearing and transcribing messages from spirit.

How did she know she was talking to Jesus? She just did. If asked to explain it, she would respond: "When you fell in love with your husband or wife, how did you know you wanted to spend the rest of your life with that person? When you bought a house, how did you know that was the house you wanted to live in? When you bought a puppy, how did you know this puppy was your puppy? You just knew. And if Jesus spoke to you, you would know that too."

Angela learned that her observing self is her spiritual self, and that her spiritual self is connected to every other being and every other thing in the universe through God's love. It is this connection which allowed her to communicate with her angels, her guides, and Jesus.

When she read *Conversations with God*[8], by Neale Donald Walsch, Angela knew that he had spoken to God and that sooner or later she would converse with God, too. She read other books by Neale and learned how to have a *Friendship with God*[9], and that there is no such thing as death, only a passing into another realm where we are *Home with God*[10].

As Angela's friendship with God developed, they began conversing regularly, and Angela knew she must share those conversations in her book.

Prior to her awakening, Angela had considered all of this very weird indeed. As she began getting used to weird, she realised it was impossible to have a deep relationship with God without being at least a little weird. She came to realise that a lot of those things which she had previously thought of as weird were really expressions of love, and they were considered weird because most people had little experience of such love.

Angela learned about God in Sunday school as a child, but even though her father had been a Congregational minister, God's love was not something that was discussed. She had completed a religion studies course some years prior to her awakening, which taught her about Hinduism,

Buddhism, Judaism, Christianity, and Islam, but God's love was not a focus of that course either. However, she did learn that each religion had a version of "Do unto others as you would have them do unto you", and she found this significant.

Angela had learned in Sunday school that God is love and after her awakening, she began to understand that love and faith were the keys to success in all things. She learned to have faith in herself, faith in the universe to bring forth her desires, and faith that God is real, and God is love.

Although her faith was not always strong, and at times she felt her faith had completely deserted her, Angela's love for God gradually increased along with her faith. Eventually she came to have great faith in God, and in her ability to hear and transcribe God's messages. She had great faith that she could be the confident, faithful, invincible beacon she had promised to be.

Tomorrow's God

God: *I love you, Angela. I just wanted to let you know that, and to let you know there are some words of wisdom in my book,* Tomorrow's God[11], *that you might like to include in your book. You know we are all one, so it is OK for me to claim credit for the book that bears Neale Donald Walsch's name as author, but you also know I appreciate both his and your efforts in helping to spread my message to the world. Thank you to both of you, and to my many other messengers. With all your help,* Tomorrow's God *will be the god of the people in the very near future.*

The Future of Education

God: *Angela, are you ready to talk about* Tomorrow's God?

Angela: Well, sort of, God. I wrote a lot of notes but I don't know quite where to start. I loved the look at the future of education. It sounds very exciting.

[The book explained that education in the New Spirituality will teach children and adults "Who They Really

Are"—"One with God" and "One with everyone and everything in the Universe". It will show children how to use the old three R's of reading, 'riting, and 'rithmetic "only as tools with which they can create" the new three R's of "reconciliation, re-creation, and reunification".]

God: *It does sound exciting, doesn't it? But there were some parts of the book you didn't agree with...*

The Future of Business and the Economy

Angela: Yes, God. I am happy to be convinced, but from my experience in our business, I just can't see how we can get to where the book states our economy will be, from where we are now. For instance, I don't think the suggestion from *Conversations with God Book 2* of writing the cost and sale price on a tag will work. We recently had an incident where we told a customer our gross margin, which is really low. They reacted badly because they were unfamiliar with comparative businesses and the overheads paid out of that margin. I just can't imagine that you can ever give a person sufficient information for them to understand the whole picture, and everyone's whole picture would be different.

The same applies to people's wages. In *CWG Book 2*, it was suggested to tell everybody everyone's wages, but people seem to have a narrow view of what others are worth and an inflated view of their own worth.

God: *Angela, I think you underestimate your fellow human. It should be possible to educate people about the whole picture without too much difficulty.*

Angela: And how do we get from here to there?

God: *In small steps, Angela—small, brave steps.*

[In *Tomorrow's God*, God said these business practices mentioned in *Conversations with God Book 2* would be examples of ways "business and the economy will become transparent".]

God: *You were right to be excited by the things you read regarding the New Spirituality, for it will hold all of the things you have been working towards—peace on Earth, and goodwill towards all people and creatures of the Earth. Have no fear. All will be well. Love will prevail.*

Angela: God, I made a note about your discussion about changing from a disposable society to a maximum use community, where we would produce *fewer consumer items* per person. This, too, is difficult to imagine. As we found in our business, people always consider the bottom line. It doesn't seem to matter that the cheapest product is going to be thrown out in one tenth of the time of the more expensive product; most people buy the cheapest. They don't seem to care that buying the cheapest is less economical in the long run, or that ultimately their own jobs may be sent off-shore in the process.

God: *Angela, you know this is changing slowly. Your government has mandated a change to more longer life lighting products because they are more efficient energy-wise. People are starting to consider how long things last, and what the effects are, not only on their long term financial situation, but also on the environment. Here again, slow steps are already happening.*

Angela and her husband, Bill, had been operating their lighting business for many years. Angela knew that in God's world anything was possible, but from her experience, she was not hopeful that she and her fellow humans could change, even with small brave steps. Then she realised if we are to bring about the world mentioned in *Tomorrow's God*, we need to base our decisions not on our experience, but on faith and love.

Consider the Consequences

The next day, Angela was walking through the mangroves when she had the urge to ask if there were any fairies in the vicinity. She had learned that fairies are like angels who look after the natural world and animals. Prior to her awakening, Angela had believed that fairies only existed in stories. Since reading Doreen Virtue's book, *Healing With the Fairies*[12], and learning from Jesus that dragonflies were the fairies' representatives in the physical world, Angela felt a strong connection to fairies—when she could bring herself to believe in them. She had many encounters with dragonflies—when she was feeling down or when she had something to celebrate—and they always lifted her spirits. Yet she was still surprised by a positive response to her question.

The fairy introduced herself as Patarina, but Angela had difficulties understanding the message, so she asked Patarina if they could continue the conversation that evening when Angela could write it down.

> Angela: Hello, Patarina. It was lovely to make your acquaintance today. Was there something you wanted to tell me?
>
> Patarina: *Yes. I wanted to ask all humans to please consider the consequences of your actions. I know sometimes you are ignorant of the consequences, but many times humans do things without ever even thinking what might happen. What might happen when you use harsh chemicals that end up in our oceans. What might happen when your plastic bags blow into the sea. What might happen when you chop down that tree, when you use up all the world's resources. When you do everything you do, consider the effect on the other animals, the other humans, the other beings who inhabit this beautiful Earth. Consider the effect on this beautiful Earth.*

Angela: Thank you, Patarina. I will try to consider the consequences of all of my actions, and ask that everyone else does as well.

Patarina: *Thank you, Angela, for helping to be a voice for the fairies, and for all the beings of the Earth.*

Angela: You're welcome, Patarina. I am happy to help. Please keep an eye on all those turtles out there, and do whatever you can to help them.

Angela had seen many dead turtles washed up on the beach, near where she lived. She knew many died because they had ingested plastic bags, mistaking them for jellyfish.

Patarina: *I will, Angela. I will pass your love and best wishes to the turtles.*

Angela: Patarina, was there anything else?

Patarina: *No, thank you, Angela. Goodbye for now.*

Angela: See you, Patarina. I hope, literally, one day.

Patarina: *One day, Angela.*

Angela hoped she and the rest of humanity would remember to consider the consequences of their actions.

Angela: God, I wanted to talk to you about the really bad dust storm we had today, across the entire east coast of Australia. I wondered if that was another of the Earth's messages to us that were spoken of in Mother Mary's book, *Mary's Message to the World*[13].

[In this book, Mary predicted an increase in earthquakes, changes to weather patterns, the extinction of many species, the melting of polar ice, and increased UFO activity, among other things. She suggested we all turn to God now.]

God: *Yes, but it is not so much a message, as a natural consequence of past actions. The Earth has created ways to shield herself from the global warming that people have created. The dust storm was a natural consequence of some of those reactions.*

Angela: God, is there anything we can do to undo what we have done to cause these and other consequences?

God: *Angela, your peace, love, healing, and joy which you send out to the world, including Mother Earth, helps, but changing people's outlook on the whole of life is really the only way to ensure a future free from such consequences. As your fairy friend pointed out to you, people need to consider the consequences of their actions.*

Angela: But, God, what about when we consider that the consequences are justified, or at least unavoidable?

For instance, it was pointed out to me that our decision to source a lot more components off-shore to help our business become profitable will add to global warming because the goods will travel by plane and because China is less likely to produce the products in an environmentally friendly way. Our business has to change to survive, and it has consequences.

God: *That's right, you will not eradicate these sorts of consequences overnight—only by small brave steps.*

Angela: Are there any small brave steps we could take now to help, God?

God: *Angela, you are tackling the problem from the macro end, not the micro end. Your book, and your loving the world will help to make people consider the way they do business. This should make it easier for businesses like yours to survive without having an adverse effect on the planet. Eventually those small brave steps, and the power of love, will lead the powers that be in China to consider the consequences of their actions also. They are beginning to now consider the consequences, but they are like you and thinking they haven't had a lot of choice.*

As you know, love conquers any problem, overcomes any difficulty. If enough people look at the problem with love, it is sure to be overcome. In the meantime, take as many small brave steps yourself, as you can.

Be Completely Honest

Angela: God, where do we begin in our business to start to take those first brave steps you spoke of?

God: *You can start by being completely honest in all of your dealings. That sounds easy, I know, but you know that complete honesty is not something that happens in any business now.*

Angela: No, God, you are right. But we know that we wouldn't have achieved many of the things we have achieved if we had been completely honest. We wouldn't have been able to use our home mortgage to prop up the business, for one thing.

God: *No, Angela, but you must start as you mean to carry on, and you can set the stage. You can be a beacon in your business as well.*

Angela: OK, God, I'll try. Anything else?

God: *No, that is the first step. You can follow this step by thinking love in all that you do in your business, and asking: 'What would love do now?' That will always see you in the right direction.*

God is Life

Angela: God, getting back to *Tomorrow's God*[14], I too, felt empowered, and befriended when I read the part where the words God and Life are interchangeable. I now know that this energy called God or Life can be used at any time as a powerful tool to create the experiences I desire, becoming my greatest friend in the process. And as I, too, am Life, I am also God.

When I think of my relationship with God in this way, I feel as though we can't help but create the peace, harmony, and respect for all life we so desire.

God: *That's right, Angela. You are a child of God, and can achieve all of your desires, but when others begin to see that God is Life, and Life is God, they will begin to help you to achieve your desires. It will have a snowball effect. You surely cannot fail.*

Angela: Oh, God, I hope so.

There's Enough

Angela: I wanted to ask about "There's enough." I have found lately that there isn't enough time or money to do what I want to do. What can I do to experience this truth?

God: *You need to believe it to experience it. You can't experience a truth if you don't believe it. You experience what you believe in. You need to believe that there's enough and enough is what there will be. Time is not your master; you are its master.*

Angela: That would be great, but how can I make that my reality?

God: *As with all things, believe and it is so. You are a creative being. You can create the experiences you desire. If you wish time to be your servant, ask and you shall receive. Believe and it is so. You can know that time is flexible, as you have been told previously. You can achieve a great deal in a short space of time. But you can't keep looking at your watch and then expect time to wait for you. Live as if there is enough time. This means only use a watch or clock when it is absolutely necessary.*

Otherwise follow your feelings, your intuition, and you can become the master of time. You can be the master of time in every second of every day of every week of every month of ever year. You are a master. Act and believe like one and all will be well.

Angela: Thanks, God. I'll give it a try, but it is hard to avoid the reminders of time when you have a grandfather clock chiming on the quarter hour.

God: *Yes, that does make it more difficult, but not impossible. You can stretch time, but only in quarter hour lots. This makes it more hard work for you. If you stop the chiming, you would find it easier to stretch time as you require it. Remember though that you have a universe working to bring you all of your desires. If you desire time to be stretched, the universe must find a way to bring you that desire. You just need to have faith.*

Who Feels the Love?

Angela: God, I wanted to talk about what I was reading today in *Tomorrow's God*, about you being in everything, and the conversation I had with you about how you feel my love.

I said to you yesterday that I could feel your love, and you said you could feel mine. I asked how you feel it, and you said the same way as I do, that you feel my vibrational energy. I was thinking today about the fact that you are in everything, but that you are an entity which is distinct from everything as well. So when I send you my love and you feel my vibrational energy, do you feel it as the distinct God-self or the everything God-self or both?

God: *Well, that is a very good question. You are right that I do have an existence that is distinct from everything, as well as an existence that is everything, and the answer is that, just as you can feel my love in every part of your being, I can feel your love in every part of my being. So when you send me love, all of my being feels it.*

Angela: God, I am aware of you and your love, and you are aware of me and my love, but what about the beings that you are? Are they aware of the love I send to you?

God: *Well, Angela, some are and some aren't. Just as you were reading in* Tomorrow's God—*there is a cycle of evolution from totally aware of the system, to totally self-aware, back to aware of the system again. Those entities that are more self-aware and have lost awareness of the all, the system, they will not be as aware of the love that the system feels. The more self-aware and less system-aware, the less they will be aware of your love. The less self-aware, and more system-aware, the more they will be aware of your love.*

Angela: I did find it exciting to think that my love reaches all of your creation, in other words, all of the universe. That seems pretty amazing to me.

God: *It is amazing, Angela. Love never ceases to amaze.*

Evolution

Angela: I have one important question, God, regarding evolution. You talked about everything being alive and some being more self-aware than others. Is it possible to know which creatures are self-aware, and can that determine whether they should be eaten or not? For if a creature considers itself only as part of the whole system, it wouldn't seem so bad to change its form to that of food; whereas if it was self aware, it may prefer to stay in its present form. Perhaps this could be the deciding factor.

God: *Yes, Angela. This could work, but I am not prepared to divulge that information now, because it may be taken out of context. If I say that, as an example, all snails, for instance, are not self-aware, might it not lead to people collecting and eating all of the snails to eat? When a change in people's view of life occurs, when people start looking to preserve all of life, then this information will be revealed. Those who are ready to receive the information and use it wisely will be given it.*

Knowing Tomorrow's God

Angela: God, I would love it if everyone could know the God I have come to know, the God that destroys nothing, rejects nothing, punishes nothing; to know that God is love, God is freedom, God is joy, God is peace, and God is unity.

God: *I would love it too, Angela, and you can help with your book. Have faith in your ability to share your love and light with all the world. Your book will shine the light on your love, and my love, and others will take up the challenge. The first small brave step will be followed by a second small brave step, and soon the New Spirituality will be a reality.*

Angela: I also loved the fact that you said in *Tomorrow's God* to look "to all sources, and even to all of Life, for your definition and experience of the Divine", and "The living of your own life writes the book of your most sacred truth". This is confirmation that God is in all of life, but first and foremost within our own selves.

You also confirmed something I had thought: "humanity cannot continue to resolve twenty-first century dilemmas with first century guidelines".

God is Everything

Angela: It was great that you said in *Tomorrow's God* that it is impossible to have anything that is not God. This should get rid of Satan forever, God.

God: *That's right, Angela. For if God is everything, God is Satan as well. But you know the story of the friendly soul. Satan is just another friendly soul, and God is there too.*

Angela had learned about the friendly soul in Neale Donald Walsch's *Conversations with God* books, which told the story of two souls in heaven discussing their next life on Earth together. The friendly soul volunteered to do something 'bad' to the other soul, so the other soul could experience itself as forgiving or some other aspect of divinity.

New Spirituality Study Group

Angela: There is so much in *Tomorrow's God*, but before I forget, I was thinking of taking up your challenge of starting an informal study group in the New Spirituality. I saw a documentary recently in which people were debunking alien abduction stories because they reckon that these victims were being coerced by the power of hypnotic suggestion. They said that anyone who goes to another person for an expert opinion is already in a suggestible state. I felt like the documentary was somehow meant for me to get something out of it, but I'm not sure what exactly. What do you think, God? Could it be that I need to be careful not to coerce people, even accidentally, into my way of thinking?

God: *That is right, Angela. People can be easily suggestible, depending on their state of mind at the time. If you just think of yourself as no more special than anyone else in the group, and ensure that everyone else thinks the same—that everyone's opinion is valid, everyone's thoughts are to be valued and honoured, and everyone is special, you should be able to ensure this doesn't happen.*

Angela: The other thing the documentary touched on was cults, and I suppose it is possible that some may think of this as a new cult, where people are brainwashed.

God: *Well, we do want people to be brainwashed to a certain extent. We want people to wash away the attitudes that are causing them and society unhappiness and disharmony, and to embrace the New Spirituality concepts of love, freedom and unity. But you are right to be concerned, and you need to be careful to ensure that everyone has free will to think as they choose. Remember that free will is paramount.*

Meditation, Eating, Exercising

Angela: And God, about your suggestion of us making a start towards the New Spirituality by meditating regularly, and changing our attitude to our bodies by eating better and exercising more—this is always a tricky one in our busy world.

God: *Yes, Angela, it is hard, but it is possible to change your priorities. You know that it is possible to turn off the TV and go for a walk. It is possible to prepare some more time-consuming healthy meals at the weekend and freeze them, or to eat more raw foods—salads and the like. If you move your body up the list of priorities, it will be easier.*

Angela: What about the idea of all things in moderation?

God: *Yes, but most people are not consuming unhealthy foods in moderation. Most people are lucky to eat one serve of fruit and one serve of vegetables per day, and animal fats are clogging up their arteries.*

Most Important Message

Angela: God, I was going to ask you: if there was one part of *Tomorrow's God* that you would want to convey, what would it be, but I just stumbled upon it now. That we are all one?

God: *Yes, Angela. That is the first lesson, the main lesson from the book. There are many lessons, as you have found, but if you embrace only one lesson, that would be it. For, from that lesson, all others flow.*

Love One Another as Yourself

Angela: Did you have anything else you wanted to point out to me?

God: *Yes, I wanted to point out the part about loving one another as yourself. You pointed out in your earlier book, that that was a common point in most of the religions you studied. This would be a good place to start, to try to bring reconciliation between the world's religions. This, at least, they can agree on, and can work from there to find other common points. With a common thread holding them together, they are more likely to be able to take more of those small brave steps towards the New Spirituality.*

Angela, as you pointed out, there are many lessons in the book, and you don't want to rewrite the whole book in your book, but you know that Tomorrow's God is the god you have come to know and love, and the god you so want to share with Bill, and others. As you read, Bill can believe in Tomorrow's God, because Tomorrow's God is another word for Life, and he already believes in life. All he needs to do is to come to realise that life is joyful, life is freedom, life is meant to be enjoyed, and life is meant to be easy. All he needs to do is to put his trust in Life to bring him all of his desires, and he, too, can experience the joy that you have experienced—the joy of Life.

Faith in Life

Angela hoped God was right, that Bill could believe in Tomorrow's God, once he realised that God was just another term for Life. Up to this point, Bill had no belief in God whatsoever. He didn't believe in even the possibility of life after death, so he found it a real challenge when Angela spoke about her conversations with spiritual beings. Angela wondered whether Bill's disconnection from God could be a major factor contributing to his repeated bouts of depression. She hoped that if he could develop a trust in Life, he could draw on that to support him in times of difficulties, just as Angela drew on her connection with God.

Although this connection became quite strong, this had not always been the case. At times, her lack of faith had interfered with this connection. She had spoken to Jesus about it.

Jesus: *Hello, Angela. I wanted to talk to you to tell you how much better you did today. Your faith has returned.*

Angela: Yes, Jesus, pretty much. A lot of that is thanks to visits from God from time to time, to remind me of his presence.

Jesus: *Yes, Angela, that has helped you, but you have turned a corner, and are on the homeward stretch as far as your faith goes. You have shown that you can have faith in God, despite the lack of much evidence. You know that God exists, because you have felt God's love, but many would still doubt God's presence. Your faith will be rewarded. Your love will be returned. All will be well.*

Angela: Thanks, Jesus. I appreciate the words of encouragement.

Jesus: *You're welcome, Angela. Keep up the good work.*

Dishonesty is Ingrained

Angela: My good work hasn't carried into every aspect of my life, Jesus. My commitment to God to try to have complete honesty in all of my business dealings hasn't borne fruit yet. I have discovered how ingrained dishonesty has become into our culture. I'm not talking major stuff, just little things like telling people on the phone that someone is in a meeting when they're not, and that sort of thing.

Jesus: *Yes, you are right. It is deeply ingrained. It will take some effort to root out dishonesty from your everyday dealings, but if you remain committed, you can achieve your goals.*

Angela: I'll try, Jesus.

Jesus: *Don't try—do, Angela.*

After loving the world, Angela spoke to God.

God: *Tonight, we should perhaps talk about business again, for, as you were telling Jesus, dishonesty is ingrained.*

Angela: Yes, God. Every aspect of business seems to be affected. Of course, anything to do with money is always 'every man, or business, for himself/itself', but even taking phone messages is difficult, as I was telling Jesus.

God: *Yes, Angela, it is difficult, because you have not yet learned that we are all one, that what you do to another, you do to yourself.*

Angela: But God, surely white lies, like saying someone

is in a meeting when they are just too busy to talk on the phone, surely those white lies don't hurt anyone.

God: *Not really, Angela, but it is the fact that the lies are systemic in business that is the problem. It means that no one stops to think of the ramifications of their dishonesty.*

Time to Wake Up

Angela: God I wanted to ask you a question. I wanted to know if in my next lifetime, I will have to be reminded of who I am, if it will take me till age 50 or so to wake up.

God: *Angela, as with all things, you can create your own reality in your next life, as you have and can in this life.*

Angela: Are you saying we are all choosing to be asleep in our lives—choosing not to know who we are?

God: *Yes, but not necessarily consciously. If you remember, one day you asked the question "What is life all about? What am I here for? Surely there is something more to life than this." It was in the asking the question that you began to wake up, that you chose to wake up. It is up to everyone to choose how they wish to live their lives—whether they want to be asleep or awake. In your higher conscious level, you always knew who you were, but on your conscious level, you were not awake.*

Angela: So is it only our conscious selves that sleeps, whereas our higher selves are always awake?

God: *That is right, Angela. In your next lifetime, if you so choose, you can be awake, and aware of who you really are throughout your lifetime.*

Angela: Why do we choose to be asleep?

God: *There are many reasons, Angela. You may choose to be asleep so that you can more easily become those things you wish to be, to experience those things you wish to experience, that you may find impossible if you were fully awake.*

Angela: I am realising that our aim is to be happy, peaceful, and to live in harmony with all of life, and that to do that we have to change the way we look at life, and God. Would it not be in everyone's interest to wake up now?

God: *Yes, Angela, and that is why there are so many of you doing just that now. There are still some things that others have to achieve before they can awaken. You are able to help them to achieve their aims and wake up, so that the changes that are needed can happen as required. Have no fear. Everything is happening as it should.*

But that doesn't mean you can rest on your laurels, Angela. Humanity needs you and those like you to carry on being a beacon, so that those who are still asleep can awaken in time. Love is the key. Have love, have faith, and all will be well. I love you, and I love the rest of my creation. Your love and my love will save the world. Your love and those like you will save the world.

Remember: love will prevail, always.

Life in the New Spirituality

Snowball of Love

God started telling Angela stories about the New Spirituality and what the world would be like in the future, leading her to believe that the messages she was recording would help change the world. God told her that a snowball of love would overtake the world, and her book would contribute to that.

> God: *Angela, I wanted to talk to you about many things, but first of all, I wanted to tell you how much I love you. I know I have told you this before, and you are not sick of hearing it, but it is not anything remarkable now. However, the depth of my love for you is so vast; the breadth of my love for you is so vast; the length of my love for you is so vast; the height of my love for you is so vast, that you cannot ever imagine its scale. But, Angela, you know that you can feel my love, now and always.*
>
> *You only need think of the word love, and you will begin to feel the love within you. Once you begin to feel that love, you feel the need to share it with others. Once you share your love with others, it is automatically returned to you.*

Our love is vast, and it is eternal, and it is infinite. It never ends. Love is all there is. Love is all that we are. We are love, you and I, and all of my creation. Angela, you can know that once you set the loving snowball in motion, it grows and grows, and there is no stopping it. Attempt to share your love with as many people and creatures of the Earth as possible, and love will grow. Your snowball of love will overtake the Earth. There will be nowhere to hide, where love will not find you.

Life in the New Spirituality

God: *Angela, I was going to tell you about the way life will be lived in the New Spirituality. Life will be more joyful, because everyone will know that they can create their own reality; everyone will know that God is with them always, and that they have many helpers—angels, guides and other helpers. They will know that their lives are based on love, and love is all around them. They will be able to feel joy in themselves by releasing joy in another. They will spread joy wherever they go.*

If they do encounter someone who is hurtful, they will know that they can control their own reactions to any hurtful comments, and they will quickly return to their state of joy again, perhaps even spreading joy to that hurtful person. Life will be wonderful.

Angela: That sounds good, God. Is there anything we can be doing now to move more quickly to that scenario?

God: *Yes, Angela, your lessons will help with that—think love before all that you do, and when faced with a decision, ask "What would love do now?" These small steps will bring everyone closer to the joy that dwells within them. Sending your love, peace, healing, and joy out into the world helps as well.*

You know that you are a beacon of love and light to all the world. Your book will help to bring this joy to all the world and allow people to see the path towards that joyful time. Your book helps light the path that dwells within each person on the Earth. Be a beacon of love and light to all the world.

Communication in the New Spirituality

God: *Now, would you like to talk about communication in the New Spirituality?*

Angela: Yes, please.

God: *Right, well, as you know, we are all one, and this is the reason you can hear our messages now.*

Angela: Yes, God.

God: *Well, Angela, in the days of the New Spirituality, everyone will be more in tune with their higher selves, their souls. They will practise meditation at least twice a day so that, in the stillness, they can listen to their higher selves. They will be able to communicate easily with all creatures and people, using the same means that you communicate with us.*

Angela: But will we be able to communicate with someone on the other side of the world like this?

God: *Yes, Angela, you will. As happens now, you get a sense someone is trying to communicate with you and you still your mind to listen. In the New Spirituality, you will get that same sense that someone wants to communicate with you, and you will then quiet your mind to listen, and communicate as you do now. In the days of the New Spirituality, you will be more practised at detecting others' energies, and so will be more easily able to discern who it is that is trying to communicate with you.*

There will be easy communication between people and creatures of the Earth, and you will be more easily able to communicate between the realms. You have already met Patarina from the Fairy realm, and have spoken to your relatives and friends who have passed over to that realm the other side of what you call death, but there are many more realms you have not yet become acquainted with. In the New Spirituality, all realms will be able to communicate much more easily.

Angela: That's great. Are all the other realms more loving than our present Earthly realm?

God: *Yes, it is only in your physical realm that people forget they are made of pure love. The other realms remember this always. There may be a few who forget to practise this, but all of the other realms are aware of this fact. Angela, do you have any questions about this communication?*

Angela: You said that I am already practising this form of communication to a certain extent, but that there is much more to learn. So teach me.

God: *But first, we need to go over a few basic rules.*

The first rule is that you never intrude on another's thoughts without their permission. With this close form of telepathy, you would easily be able to read another's thoughts, but you know yourself that you wouldn't always want another knowing what you are thinking. In the days of the New Spirituality, there will be more openness and less secrecy, so most people will not be too concerned if someone accidentally reads their thoughts, but it will be better to ask permission first.

As you have learned to ask to only communicate with guides of the highest vibration, similarly you will be able to ask to communicate with a particular person only. You would then wait for a response, so you know it is safe to listen to their thoughts.

Angela: It sounds like it might take some practice.

God: *Yes, Angela, but you are practising now. You don't perhaps have the same amount of control over your thoughts that people will have in the New Spirituality, but you are practising discerning our energies, practising listening to our thoughts, and practising sending your thoughts to us.*

Angela: Are there any other rules?

God: *Yes, another rule is that you should always protect yourself with white light before your communications.*

Angela: I don't do that now, God, though I have read that it is advised.

God: *No, Angela. Your angels and guides are protecting you now, but you know that even so, in your earlier communications, you did have a few negative energies attach to you. In the New Spirituality, there will be less negative energy around, but it will be best to always use the white light first. Just say: "I surround myself with the white light of love and divine protection", as you learned from John Edward.*

Angela had learned from books[15] and psychic development CDs[16] that this was the way John Edward, the world famous psychic medium, protected himself.

Angela: Is that all the rules?

God: *Those are the main ones, Angela.*

Angela: So, teach me.

God: *First, you need to decide who you want to talk to.*

Angela: Well, I would like to talk to a few people, but they haven't had these lessons, so how can they communicate with me?

God: *You might be surprised. You need to decide on one person. If you think of more than one person at a time, you will get mixed messages.*

Angela: I will choose my friend, Lynn.

God: *Good. Now the first thing to say is: "I would like to communicate with my friend, Lynn. I am Angela Shepherd and I seek communication at this time." Similar to what you have been doing, but it is communication you are requesting, not assistance. You now wait for a response.*
You say it.

Angela: OK, God. [Angela repeated what she had just learned.]… I heard an "Hello, Angela".

God: *Now ask permission to read her thoughts.*

Angela: Lynn, may I read your thoughts?

Lynn: *Yes, Angela, you may. Angela, I missed you so much since I left. It is good to communicate with you.*

Angela: Where are you, Lynn?

Lynn: *I am on the other side of the world from you, in downtown London.*

Angela: So, come back to Australia to visit.

Lynn: *No, you come over here.*

Angela: One day.

Angela: OK, God, that was an interesting experiment. Was Lynn conscious of that communication, or was it her higher self communicating with me?

God: *Angela, it was her higher self on that occasion, but you know that your higher self and you are one being. Lynn will be aware of the conversation at some level in her consciousness. She may not realise, however, that it was a real conversation, but perhaps will think it is just her mind playing tricks.*

Angela: This form of communication is possible now?

God: *Yes, with more people becoming aware of this ability, it will be possible to communicate with more and more people in the near future.*

Angela: Sorry, God. You've left me speechless again.

God: *That's OK. Remember if you are going to practise this, you first have to remember the rules:*
1/ First, surround yourself in white light. And
2/ Always ask permission to read the other's thoughts.

Angela: If I forget to do one of those things, can I ask in advance for protection whenever I communicate, and to be reminded to ask permission?

God: *You can ask, but it is best to follow the rules. But remember, ask and you shall receive.*

Angela: God, I wanted to ask about the negative energy that you spoke about attaching to me when I didn't surround myself in white light, even though my angels and guides were protecting me. Where did this negative energy come from?

God: *Angela, when you communicate like this, you open yourself up to allow the messages to come in. If you don't surround yourself in white light, there is a small risk of energy that is hanging around the Earth to attach itself to you inadvertently. There is a fair amount of negative energy on the Earth plane, because of the amount of fear that exists there. This will reduce drastically with the New Spirituality, but the negative energies you attracted were caused by the fear that exists there now. If you surround yourself with white light, the negative energy cannot attach itself to you because you have a layer of protection around you.*

Where is the Dividing Line?

Angela: God, I know I should mention the conversation we had earlier, when you accused me of not always believing in you. I do always believe in you, God. I just don't really understand where the dividing line is between you and me.

God: *I know, Angela. It can be a difficult concept to grasp. You know that we are one, and you know that we have individual thoughts, so you have trouble amalgamating the two concepts. You know I told you that there is no dividing line between us, and that is true. It is like you read in the book,* Home With God[17]: *it is like a wave in the ocean—there is no dividing line. Yet you are an individual, with individual thought.*

Angela: God, this is where I have difficulty. How do I know, when walking up the street, if the response is from you or my mind? I know you said that if I think love first, but if I am to treat you as a friend, a friend would just have a chat, not stop mid-chat to think love.

God: *No, you are right, but remember also that you can be, do, and have whatever you desire. If you desire to have a chat with God without your mind interfering in the answers, just ask and you shall receive. But you can know that there is no dividing line between us. We are ONE.*

Angela: OK, God. Gotcha, I think.

God: *All of this universe is made of love—all of the beings, all of the creatures, all of matter in the universe is made of love. Angela, you know that God is love, and that God created the universe. This universe is all love; there is nothing in this universe that is apart from that love. You know that we are all one—that you and I and everything, every being in this universe is one being, indivisible, yet individuated.*

Angela: I don't quite get the difference, God.

God: *I know, Angela. As was explained previously, as your leg is to your whole body, so you are to the body of God, to the body of the universe. You are an individual part of God, an individual part of the universe, yet there is no dividing line between us.*

Angela, love is the key to all things, because love is all things. Love can conquer any problem, overcome any difficulty. Love is all you will ever need.

Communicating With Other Realms

God: *Do you want to carry on our conversation about communication in the New Spirituality?*

Angela: Yes, please, God. I wanted to ask about the other realms. What are they, and do we just communicate with them the same?

God: *The realms are: the Earth plane, the Fairy realm, which includes all the other Elementals. The other Elementals include the Dragonfae that you have learned about from your cards[18], along with all of the fairies and goblins, that Bill thinks you are off with. There are a number of different beings in this realm, and I think you have found out about them from a couple of the books you have read. The next realm is the Deceased Persons realm. The next realm is where you will find the Ascended Masters, and those other beings who wish to help humanity, such as Star and Light Beings, whom you have met once, I believe. The next realm is the Angel realm, and you have spoken to a couple of those. Next are the Archangels, and then you find me.*

OK, so once you know which realm you want to talk to, you can just ask to speak to someone from that realm. If you know which being you want to talk to, you can ask to speak to that being, such that if you know their name, ask by name. But if you only know the type of being, ask for that. Ask for communication, not assistance, if that is what you're requesting. Here again, follow the rules. With higher beings, such as angels, they are less likely to be offended if you forget to ask permission, but it is polite to do so anyway.

Angela: OK, God. Sounds good.

God: *Angela, how do you think it will be to live and communicate in the New Spirituality?*

Angela: The communication will be easy but it will hold more responsibility—responsibility to control our thoughts better.

God: *That's right, Angela. You don't want to be thinking something bad about someone, and then have them hear that. How can we get around that?*

Angela: By not thinking bad thoughts about anyone, ever.

God: *Yes, that would work. But that could be tricky, couldn't it?*

Angela: Not if we remember that we are all one, so what we think about another, we are thinking about ourselves.

God: *That's right, Angela. This is the reason that this was the most important lesson in* Tomorrow's God, *and the most important lesson to teach to your children, and your children's children—we are all one.*

What you do to another, you do to yourself. What you think of another, you think of yourself. We are all one.

Communicating With Animals

Angela: God, I wanted to ask about communicating with animals. We talked about communicating with people and other realms, but what about other entities in this physical realm? Is the communication the same with animals and plants, as it is with humans? We just follow the same rules, and just communicate the same?

God: *That's right, Angela. Communication between people and animals will be easy in the New Spirituality. You can do it now, as you have discovered with the dragonflies. I know that you had tried other times and not succeeded, but that could be because you didn't know to ask for permission to read the being's thoughts. Once you ask permission, and receive a positive response, the other's thoughts will become obvious to you. You can give it a try with Cassie. Just remember the rules. The same would apply with talking to plants and crystals, and any being on the Earth, or in any of the realms for that matter.*

Angela went away and practised what she had learned with her dog, Cassie. She telepathically asked a sleeping Cassie if there was anything she would like to change about her life now. The response she received of "more food" certainly sounded like the response a Dobermann would give.

God: *I wanted to ask you how your practice communications went with Cassie?*

Angela: Well, it was a brief conversation, and I wasn't certain that it was Cassie's thoughts I was getting. But it was OK.

God: *Angela, you should try it in another room from Cassie. You will be more able to determine a change in the energy you are receiving, when you feel Cassie's sweet energy that you previously described. It will be easier to notice the difference in energy when she is not right there with you. Once you are confident in the feeling that you feel, when you know that it is her energy, you will be more able to discern this energy when it is replicated in a face to face conversation.*

When Jesus first communicated with her, Angela had remarked that his energy seemed sweet, just like Cassie's.

God: *Did you have any more questions?*

Angela: Well, there was one that came to me. You may think it silly.

God: *Not likely, Angela.*

Angela: Well, I wondered: if I was faced with a ferocious wild animal, like a polar bear, would it still be wise to open a conversation with "May I read your thoughts?" or should I go straight to "Do you intend to eat me?"

God: *That is a good question. Let love be your guide, as in all things. This includes love for yourself and your body. Your feelings will tell you the right answer. Your love will tell you the right answer. "What would love do now?" is still the best question to ask in any situation, but in the circumstances you described, I would ask it very quickly.*

Angela later learned about people who offered courses in communicating telepathically with animals. When she attended those courses, she discovered that, here too, love was the key.

Seeing into Other Realms

God: *Angela, I wanted to tell you a few more things about the New Spirituality. I wanted to let you know that in the New Spirituality, you would be able to not only hear into this realm but see into it as well.*

Angela: How would that work, God? Into the spirit realm?

God: *That's right, into all the other realms. You will be able to see the fairies you speak to, speak face to face with the dragonfae, see once again your deceased parents, see the beauty of the angels and archangels, and the figures of the ascended masters.*

Angela: Will this be only when we are speaking to them or will there be a lot of ghosts hanging around?

God: *No, Angela, it will be only when you wish to communicate with them, or they wish to communicate with you.*

Angela: What about those deceased people who aren't aware they are dead, as we hear about from time to time now? Will we be seeing a lot of ghosts and such?

God: *No, Angela, in the New Spirituality, there will be fewer lost souls, as everyone will be able to see them and help them cross over, whereas now it is only a few who can see and understand what they need.*

Angela: That sounds good. Is that something I can start to practise now, too?

God: *Angela, your clairvoyance is not so well developed as your clairaudience. You can practise it now, but you may have a way to go before you perfect it. You can start by going through the beings that you wish to talk to in meditation. Ask to communicate with them as you have learned, and ask if they are able to show themselves to you. Beings such as the fairies and dragonfae are selective as to who they allow to see them. In the New Spirituality, they will have developed a trust in the human species, whereas now they are quite wary because of past hurts. Have patience with them, and yourself, and you will succeed in the end.*

You had some questions for me?

Angela: Yes, God. I wanted to know a bit more about the star beings and light beings you spoke of when discussing the realms.

God: *Well, Angela. You can know that they are beings who live in another area of the universe. They know of your plight to try to rid the Earth of negativity, so they have volunteered to help.*

Angela: But if they live in the physical universe, do they not live in the physical realm?

God: *No, Angela. They live in another realm altogether. As you learned from reading the* Conversations With God *books, it is not always a good idea to know all of the information about other realms and other beings. It is far better to concentrate your efforts and your energies on your own realm, on your own area of influence.*

Angela: OK, God, for now. I might try to glean a bit more information later, perhaps a bit at a time.

God: *You can try, Angela. You know that I have said, "Ask and you shall receive."*

Angela: That's right, God. Does that mean if I really press you, you have to tell me?

God: *Yes, but remember to be careful what you ask for, because you just might get it.*

Angela: OK, God. Thanks. My other question was relating to the appearance of spirits—when we are communicating with them. I wondered if spiritual beings can choose the form they show to us. For instance, can my mother show me a middle aged form, as opposed to her age when she passed away?

God: *That is right, Angela. Deceased persons will generally try to show you the appearance with which you will feel most comfortable. The beings in the Fairy realm generally have a more fixed appearance, but some beings here, too, can change their appearance.*

Starting the Snowball of Love Rolling

God: *The next thing I wanted to talk about was what will be happening in your collective futures. I mentioned we would talk about the timing of the changes coming to the world with the New Spirituality, and you can know that the timing of the changes will largely depend on you.*

Angela: On me, God?

God: *Not you personally, Angela, though you will help achieve these goals, but you as a collective of humans on your planet. Your commitment will determine the speed with which you achieve them. Your ability to work together will determine how quickly you get there. As you learned from* Tomorrow's God[19], *I am calling on all the people of the Earth to become part of the "humanity team" that will work together to achieve the small brave steps towards the New Spirituality.*

Share your love and light and you help light the path to the New Spirituality. You can help start the snowball rolling and gather lots of people who can help you achieve your goals. This all sounds like a big responsibility, not only for you but for the rest of the humanity team, but remember that you are all one and you can work together to lighten the load on each individual. Remember, you have many helpers.

To start progressing towards the New Spirituality, I suggest beginning with the New Spirituality study groups discussed in Tomorrow's God *and earlier in your book. Once you have a loyal band of humanity team members in that group, you will find teachers among you who can educate others in what they have learned. The teachers can speak with the age groups with which they feel most comfortable. Informal education sessions, which are fun for both adults and children alike, can be in place long before there is any change in government bodies required to change curriculums.*

Once you start the ball rolling, opportunities to advance the humanity team's efforts will present themselves, and the team may expand, provided there is a firm commitment.

Angela: How can we be sure that the snowball continues to roll in the right direction, God?

God: *Angela, your angels and guides are helping you with this, but provided that love is your guide at all times, you cannot fail. If you remember to ask: "What would love do now?" you are sure to succeed to keep the snowball heading in the right direction. You know you can always call on me for assistance.*

Angela: OK, God. That sounds like a good plan, and it sounds so positive.

God: *That's right, Angela. If you keep a positive attitude, you are more likely to achieve your goals more quickly.*

Angela: Was there anything else, God?

God: *Yes, Angela. I wanted to let you know that it really was me giving you a loving vibration today and not your imagination. You are right that you should have more faith by now, but it is understandable. As you read in* The Lightworker's Way[20], *your ego self is continually trying to separate us.*

Angela: How can I control my ego self better, God?

God: *Angela, as long as you remember to think love, and you regularly meditate, you will stay in touch with your higher self, so these attempts to separate us won't succeed. Ask, and you shall receive.*

Angela: OK God. I ask to be forever connected to you—never to lose my connection, to always remember your love and that it is real, and to always remember that we are one.

God: *Good, Angela, and so it shall be.*

Their conversation continued the next day.

Angela: Hello, God. I got the urge to talk to you while making the bed again. There must be something about bed making that is conducive to spiritual communication.

God: *It doesn't require much thought, Angela. It is like an active meditation. Did you have something you wanted to discuss?*

Angela: No, I just felt close to you, and wanted to talk to you. Did you have something you wanted to discuss?

God: *No, I just felt close to you and wanted to talk to you but we could discuss your movement towards the New Spirituality.*

Angela: OK, God.

God: *Angela, now that you have made the decision to go forward, this is what will happen. You will be busy with your book and your business, but it would be good if you can also start your New Spirituality study group.*

Go now, Angela, and enjoy the rest of your day. You know that you can talk to me at any time. We both were in the mood for a formal chat, so I called this meeting, so to speak, but you can talk to me anytime—discuss your problems, your difficulties, your joy, your likes, your dislikes. Remember that although I am God, I am still your friend, and I can be an ear to hear your cares and triumphs without judgement. I love you, Angela, and want only the best for you, so feel free to call on me any time for a chat.

Living In Harmony

God: *I wanted to tell you that in the New Spirituality, there will be much rejoicing when the Earth becomes a place where people and animals live in harmony. You will be one of those rejoicing when all the people of the Earth treat the animals with respect because they realise that we are all one.*

Angela: Yes, that would be good.

God: *Angela, the people of the Earth will realise that we are all one. They will not want to eat the sentient beings that they have been eating. They won't want another being to suffer so that they may eat. There will be more vegetarians and many more vegetarian products. You will find it easier to find healthy food to eat, because everyone will be eating healthy vegetarian food.*

Angela: Sounds good, God. What will happen to all the farmed animals? They can't just roam free or they will jeopardise the native animals.

God: *Angela, all of the animals of the Earth will have the same value in the New Spirituality. One will not have more value than another because it is native or because it is edible. People will find ways to limit the effects that their domesticated animals have on their environment. With more people eating a vegetarian diet, there will be no need for the breeding and mass production of food animals. They will live to old age and die natural deaths.*

You know that where there is a will, a way will be found to respect all life without jeopardising the environment and habitats of the native animals. All of life has value. People will come to realise this, and will work hard to ensure that the domesticated animals are given the same respect as the native animals, whilst preserving their habitats.

The oceans will start to recover. People will have more concern for where all of their waste products end up. Recycling will take on new meaning and every item will be valued. There will be less rubbish and therefore, less rubbish that can end up in the oceans.

Mother Earth on which your lives depend will feel loved again. She will begin to forgive past wrongs as, in the New Spirituality, people will have respect for her as well. She will respond with love for all beings of the Earth. She will have fewer reasons to create the devastation that she has created in recent times. There will be mutual respect between the Earth and all of her inhabitants.

Life will truly be wonderful for all the inhabitants of the Earth. As we discussed before, everyone will communicate freely between the species. Humans will have no more reason to fear the animals, and the animals will have no more reason to fear humans. Each will know what the other is doing, so there will be no surprises.

Angela: It sounds wonderful, God, but like a lot of small brave steps away.

God: *Angela, it needn't be. As the snowball rolls, there will be no stopping it.*

Angela: What about those people you spoke of, who are

not ready to wake up yet? Won't they stop the snowball?

God: *They will be in the minority, Angela, and increasingly so. Have no fear. The New Spirituality will take over the Earth. Love will prevail, always. As long as all you do is based on love, you cannot fail.*

Angela, go forth and be a beacon of God's love and light to all the world. You can be a voice now to work towards the New Spirituality and help bring about this new world.

Angela, in the New Spirituality, all the people and animals of the Earth, and the Earth itself, will live in peace and harmony. People will love each other easily. There will be no embarrassment in hugging, kissing, or making love. Love in all its forms will be seen as the natural part of joyful life that it is.

People will communicate easily without words, so there will be no divide between people of different tongues. Although different cultures will still exist, all people's cultures will be respected, and people will be eager to learn the wonderful things about other cultures without necessarily wanting to take those things into their own culture.

There will be much joy, as everyone will think love in all that they do. There will be much joy, because people will be free to be who they really are, and, as we learned earlier, freedom leads to joy. Freedom is joy.

Angela, the New Spirituality is only so many small brave steps away. The people of the Earth can quickly move towards that day, once they set their minds to it. The snowball of love will take over the world.

Angela, when the New Spirituality is in place, there will be much rejoicing because life will be so much better for everyone, because there will be less fear and more love. As you have found out, Angela, when you think love more often, you are much happier.

Angela: That's right, God.

God: *Well, everyone will be thinking love more often, so everyone will be happier. It will be much easier to bring out the joy in others because it will be closer to the surface of all the people and creatures of the Earth. Because there will be more love, there will be even more love. For, as you have found, when you love the world and your love is returned tenfold, the more love you send out, the more you get back; the more joy you release in another, the more you release in yourself.*

Everyone will be happy. Everyone will live happy, loving, joyful lives, and you can help start people towards that path towards the New Spirituality. Your book will, itself, release the joy in some people, which will help start the snowball rolling.

Angela: That would be good, God.

God: *It would be, Angela. You can also help with your New Spirituality study group, which will begin to spread the word of love wherever its members go. It will be an exciting time for you, Angela, as you help the world move towards this new age.*

Miraculous Healings

Angela: God, I have a question about the lead up to the New Spirituality. There presumably will be a lot of people who now suffer some affliction, who decide they don't need it anymore. I wondered if there will be paraplegics who start to walk, and deaf people who start to hear, or were these afflictions conditions that the higher selves of these people have chosen for their life lessons?

God: *There will be some of both categories of people. There will be a lot of miraculous healings in the coming days, so you would be wise to expect that, but there will be some people who wish to keep their afflictions.*

Angela: This could be painful for those people who have to accept that a miracle cure is not for them, when they see it in others.

God: *Yes, Angela, but no more painful than some of the lessons you endure and benefit from. I would suggest to everyone that every situation can be cherished. Make the most of every situation you find yourself in. Love will see you through all difficulties. Communication with their higher selves during meditation will allow people to understand the wishes of their higher selves, and the lessons they are hoping to learn.*

All of life can be cherished if it is looked at with love, Angela, even life with afflictions. Many people have defied their doctors' predictions and created wonderful, or at least, useful lives for themselves, despite, or often because of afflictions. Steven Hawking is one notable example.

Angela: I hope all of these people enjoy their lessons more than I have done.

God: *They will if they look at them with love, and if they look for the joy in every situation, for you know that joy can be found in every situation. You also know that you can create your own reality, so you can create a happy, joyful life, including afflictions.*

Resolving Differences

God: *Angela, you know that in the New Spirituality everyone will get along with each other, with the Earth, and the creatures of the Earth. When everyone gets along, there will be new ways of resolving differences.*

Angela: That's good. The current ways are rather painful. Will we be able to do away with lawyers?

God: *No, Angela, but lawyers will be used in a different way. They will be used to draft bills of rights and new laws, but there will be less need for lawyers. No one will be wanting to sue another, for as you have found in your experience, the only people who win out of a lawsuit are the lawyers.*

But there will be new ways of co-existence. There will be greater collusion between parties to arrive at a negotiated settlement between all concerned. People will be much more able to see the other's point of view, because they will see themselves in that position. They will be able to empathise with the other person. Angela, there will be agreements drawn up for future generations—not to limit anyone's freedom, but to allow people of future generations to understand those conditions which were important to their ancestors. But these agreements will be flexible because it will be understood that conditions change, and what is right for one generation, will not be right for all the generations to come.

Angela, how does that sound?

Angela: It sounds like a society that will allow more freedom for everyone, whilst still respecting the wishes of everyone.

God: *That is right. Compromises may be necessary, but everyone will see the necessity for them, and accept them as such, because they will be able to see both sides of the argument.*

Employment

God: *Also there will be much rejoicing, because everyone will be happy in their roles in society. No job will be considered lowly. In fact, those jobs, which may now be considered such, will be highly prized, because they are service jobs, and service to others will be more of a joy in the New Spirituality because people will understand that through service, they can bring out the joy in others, and thus the joy in themselves.*

Once the New Spirituality is in place, there will be no need for people to work at any job that they don't want to. There will be much more sharing of wealth, and remember that we discussed in Tomorrow's God *that wealth will be defined differently, as access to things rather than ownership of things. This redistribution of wealth means it will be easier for each person to have those things they require for survival and fulfilment. Money will not be such an issue as it is today. The word work may be taken out of your vocabulary and replaced with another word, like occupation, which would be used to describe the work a person does in order to fulfil themselves, and perhaps to receive an income.*

There will be much more equality in employment. There will still be managers and workers, but they will each see themselves as equals, just with different roles in the business. Everyone will enjoy their occupation, for there won't be anything that will force a person to work in a position they don't enjoy.

Angela: But God, even people who really enjoy their jobs now have the odd day when they'd rather be doing something else, but feel obliged to go to work.

God: *Yes, Angela, and that obligation which now makes a person go to work grudgingly, will, in the time of the New Spirituality, see people going to work because they are happy to be of service to their fellow human (or animal, as the case may be). With more honesty and equality, if a person becomes disenchanted with their employment, they will work with others in their environment to find the best solution for all concerned. When people are more in touch with their higher selves, they will have a better view of their long term and short term goals in life, and a better understanding of how their present roles would help to achieve their goals. Employment will naturally be more joyful.*

Angela: That sounds great, God. Thank you, once again, for sharing this with me.

God: *You're welcome, Angela. I want your book to excite people about the possibilities that await them, so they will work towards the New Spirituality and bring it about more quickly, which will be better for everyone.*

Stewardship

God: *Now, would you like to talk about stewardship?*

Angela: Of course I would.

God: *Angela, stewards are what I am hoping you and the rest of your species will become in the New Spirituality, and in the not too distant future. I would love it if you could all become stewards of the Earth. This doesn't mean, as some of your earlier texts and religions have said, that you have dominion over the Earth, but that you are assigned the task of caring for the Earth, just as the beings of the Fairy realm do. But, whereas the Fairy realm has limited power in the physical world, humans have the power to change the world—for the better or for the worse.*

Up to date, your species has not had a good record in this regard, and most changes to the Earth have been to its detriment, which is why Mother Earth has been reacting to these changes with defensive actions of her own. But you know, Angela, that you and all the people of the Earth can be, do, and have whatever you desire. If you all desire a way to live in harmony with Mother Earth and her inhabitants of every kind, then the universe must bring you a way to do that.

Angela: Well, God, I for one, would love to find a way in which we could all contribute to change for the better, rather than change for the worse.

God: *That's good, Angela, but you know that you have the power to do that every day you are on the Earth.*

The first step would be to think love for the Earth and all of her inhabitants, as you have already been doing on a daily basis.

The second step would be to consider the consequences of your actions—the consequences to the Earth and other inhabitants.

Also you can start to put your mind to ways to change the world. Already some people are converting to solar powered hot water, and solar power which feeds into your electricity grid. This all reduces the reliance on coal-fired power stations. Your government is encouraging this to a limited extent. They could do more by providing more incentive for people changing to solar. More could also be done to establish wind power, wave power, and other natural sources of energy to provide electricity.

As you know, motor vehicles are a large cause of pollution on the Earth. More government encouragement of public transport could see this reduced. There is much the individual can do by considering the use of vehicles that is required in all that you do and buy. Buy local goods, for instance, that haven't travelled by polluting vehicles. The individual could reduce their own vehicle trips by car pooling, cycling, walking, by working locally. All it takes is a bit of thought, and there is much each individual could accomplish.

Angela, you, yourself, could do more to reduce your carbon footprint, by using your car less, travelling to work together with Bill only, working at home on your VPN more, and saving a trip altogether.

Angela: That would suit me, God.

God: *I know, Angela. All it would take is a bit more thought and planning.*

Angela: OK, God.

God: *Also, Angela, reducing the amount of rubbish in your environment will reduce the amount of rubbish that ends up polluting the oceans, and causing your friends— the turtles, among others—difficulties you already know about. I would suggest that every human on the planet could contribute less rubbish.*

Angela: God, I was remembering back to my childhood. I remembered that Mum and Dad used to wash out plastic bags and then hang them out to dry, to recycle them.

God: *Yes, Angela. Back then plastic bags were not so plentiful, so they were more frugal in their use of them.*

There is much that can be done, both on the individual level, the corporate level, and the government level to bring about a more harmonious relationship with the Earth and her inhabitants.

Once your New Spirituality groups are up and

running and there are a number of members, you will find there will be those among you who are qualified to start a think tank for stewardship of the Earth. This think tank could come up with suggestions for ways in which people can improve their contribution to stewardship, but also suggestions for ways that governments and corporations could improve their contributions as well.

Gratitude

Angela: By the way, God, I said a few prayers of gratitude. Thank you, God, for that idea. Gratitude for something on its way to me, made me feel wonderful, I guess because it became more real to me because of the gratitude.

God: *That's right, Angela. It became more real to you, and because of that, it became more real to the universe, which is bringing it to you. Your desire will come to you that much more quickly now.*

Angela: God, one of the things I was giving gratitude for was for the New Spirituality coming to the Earth. So if a lot of people start offering the same prayer of gratitude, does that mean it will increase the speed of that coming, by the number of people offering that prayer?

God: *That's right, Angela. The more people giving a prayer of gratitude for the coming to pass of the New*

Spirituality, the more the universe believes it, and the faster it comes.

Angela: If I make one of my prayers of gratitude about increasing the number of people offering prayers of gratitude for the New Spirituality, the number of people offering prayers will increase, and this will bring the desired result?

God: *Yes, Angela. Well done. You are starting to understand the idea behind creating your own reality— the reality you desire. Keep focused on your desires with a positive outlook, and you cannot fail.*

Highly Evolved Beings

God: *Angela, with the New Spirituality there will be much rejoicing, because everyone will have their joy much closer to the surface, so everyone will easily be able to bring out the joy in each other, and you know that everyone will be working in jobs they enjoy, and people will all get along with each other, with other creatures, and with the Earth herself. But there will also be much to rejoice about, because people from this planet will start to communicate with people from other planets.*

Beings from more advanced planets have been watching your planet with interest as you move closer to the New Spirituality. They are waiting until the time is right for communication to commence. Once love is the dominant force on your planet, beings from other planets will be happy to communicate with you on your planet. There is much the people of your planet can learn from those beings, once they are certain you are ready.

Angela: It sounds exciting, God.

God: *Angela, what do you think they will be able to teach you?*

Angela: I don't know, God.

God: *Angela, they can teach you how to be.*

Angela: How to be what?

God: *How to be, Angela—how to be a more highly evolved being: how to communicate, how to live, and how to love as a highly evolved being. There is much they can teach you, when you are ready.*

There are exciting times ahead for your planet, and these exciting times are a mere snowball's roll away.

Once the New Spirituality is in place, and everyone is more loving, and you are communicating with beings from other planets, your progress will be even faster. For they will teach you how to be more highly evolved. They will patiently show you the best and easiest ways to move forward.

Because everyone will be more empathetic and able to

understand other points of view, everyone will live in peace and harmony. Everyone will want to reduce their negative impacts on their environment and will want to buy local products and work locally as much as possible. Communities will be stronger, as people get to know their neighbours. Bartering will be common practice as people try to recycle more, and they will realise that their old rubbish might be just what someone else is looking for.

Buildings will be much more environmentally sound, just like the one you saw recently that recycles all of its waste water and grows its own plants in a closed cycle. These buildings will also be self-sufficient with solar cells and other renewable energy for the small amount consumed.

Because recycling will be popular, buildings won't be pulled down to construct new dwellings, but there will be a lot of adaptation of old dwellings to allow for environmentally sound properties to be incorporated into older buildings.

In the New Spirituality, and moving more into it, architects, builders and home owners will be looking for the best way to use the resources that are available, and to reuse recycled items. As people consider how they can preserve life on the planet, they will be looking for ways to keep the trees in the forest, and reuse other materials which would otherwise become waste. New industries will spring up in recycling products. Any new industries will need to be powered by non-polluting, renewable energy.

The chief lesson of the New Spirituality is that we are

all one. If you can keep this in mind, think love and live in the moment, you have the essential building blocks for the New Spirituality. But, in order to build a house, you need more than foundations; you need colours and lights. You have to have something to build upon from those foundations. Angela, you need to have more information to be able to build a whole culture. Granted, those basic blocks will go a long way towards where you want to go, but you need more. Books, religions, and shared current knowledge will provide those colours and lights—the extra information you need to build a culture based on love. Angela, do you understand now why you need this extra information?

Angela: Yes, I think so, God. To allow us to overcome challenges that may present themselves. To know which way to turn when we come to a crossroads. And to help us find our way to the New Spirituality in the quickest, most efficient way possible.

God: *That's right, Angela.*

Love

God: *Angela, I want to talk about love.*

You know that, in the lead-up to the New Spirituality, love will become the dominant force in the world. Love will be on everyone's minds and in everyone's thoughts. Once the New Spirituality is here, and it has overtaken the world, love will be obvious from one end of the globe to the other.

For you know that love surrounds you now; love is in all things and all that matters; love is in all matter. But in the future, everyone will realise this. Everyone will think: "What will love do now?" when faced with any decisions. Everyone will think love, be love, and act with love in all that they do. Love will be the "be all" and "end all". Love will be the alpha and the omega, and everything in between. Love will take the world to new heights, and beings from other planets will help you move the world to even greater heights.

All will be well. Everyone will have a close connection to God, just as you do now—even more so. Everyone will use their internal guidance system—God's guidance system—to help them with every decision. Love will, indeed, rule the world.

Love is all there is, Angela. A lot of people experience only fear, but even their fear is a form of love. For God so loved the world, that God allowed the people of the world to experience fear, so they would then truly understand its opposite, which is love. But having experienced fear, they need experience it no more. People can realise that there is nothing to fear, but fear itself. Love is the only reality.

Hold fast to my love, to the love that dwells within yourselves, the love that dwells within every being, within all of my creation, and fear will become a thing of the past. Hold fast to my love, and love will soon rule the world.

Healing

God: *In the New Spirituality, everyone will understand that they are one with all that is, with all of God's creation. Everyone will be able to use their own natural healing abilities to heal themselves and assist others to heal themselves. As you discovered with your healing course and the books you have read, the body has amazing healing abilities. You discovered this recently with your leg injury, and will soon learn of its ability to heal your thyroid.*

You know that your healing journey has been a process that has taken a few years. You know that your NAET[21] (Nambudripad's Allergy Elimination Techniques) treatments, your Quantum Bioenergetics[22], and your Journey[23] work have all contributed to the health you experience today. You also know that avoiding chemicals in your foods, by trying to only eat organic and as little processed foods as possible has also helped you.

With New Spirituality, more people will be discovering alternative healing techniques. Many have already experienced Reiki, another form of healing that benefits many. As the New Spirituality comes into play, everyone will want to work on their psychological issues with programs like The Journey, because they will understand that emotional issues can cause physical issues, just as you and Brandon Bays have done.

People will understand that a way to begin tackling their psychological, emotional, and physical issues is regular meditation. Only from this calm centre can you begin to heal all of your issues. People will have more respect for their bodies and will be more careful with what they put into them. Just as they have more respect for all of life, they will have more respect for their own lives as well. There will be more calm, healthy people in the years just ahead. They will understand that before they love another, they need to love themselves, and they will understand that meditation and respecting their bodies will help them to do that.

Now that the Earth is filled with calm, healthy people, they will have fewer of their own problems to worry about, and can concentrate on alleviating the suffering of others, both in the form of sending and offering healing and love to others, but also in the form of physical and material assistance to all those less fortunate than themselves.

Who is God?

God: *In the New Spirituality, everyone will know that we are all one and that everyone is connected to each other through their connection to God. They will know they can communicate directly with God if they wish, but because they understand that we are all one, they will see God in everyone they meet, in everything they see. When another person talks to them with love, they will understand that it is God talking to them. They will understand that God talks to everyone all of the time, not only from within, but from without as well. When they see someone acting with love, they will see God. When they see someone being love, they will see God. When they look at all of God's creation, they will see God.*

For God so loved the world, that God filled the world with love. Everyone needs only to be the love they are in order to experience that love. Everyone can be the love they know they are by thinking love, by asking "What would love do now?" when faced with any decision, and by acting with love in all they do. Everyone will know that when they do these things, when they are being love, they are being God. Everyone will know themselves as God.

Look for the Blessings

God spoke with Angela again the next evening. She had attended a Dance of the Goddess workshop that afternoon. Although she had enjoyed the experience, she wasn't sure it was beneficial. It was a women-only workshop which allowed expression and honouring of the feminine within, in the form of dance, discussions, and artwork. When talking to God, Angela realised that it was more beneficial than she had first recognised.

> Angela: Hello, God. I love you. I just wanted to let you know that, after my afternoon of Dance of the Goddess with all those lovely women, I am thinking of you and feeling your energy as more female for the first time, God. I guess that is a reflection of honouring the feminine in me.
>
> God: *Yes, Angela. That's right. You spent the afternoon honouring the Goddess in yourself and your classmates. It*

is only natural that you would be more in tune with the feminine in me as well. How did you enjoy your day?

Angela: I enjoyed it, God, but I did feel something holding me back a bit.

God: *Yes, Angela. You have many inhibitions which have been built up over many years. This afternoon allowed you to let go of some of those inhibitions, but you cling to some for protection, so you don't feel exposed. Each time you attend something like this, where you have to step outside of your comfort zone, you slowly chip away at your inhibitions. You are wondering whether to include this conversation in your book, and it would be a good idea to. It demonstrates what I was talking about in* Tomorrow's God, *about experiencing other spiritual practices. You may not agree with everything that is said or done, but you will take something away from each of these things you attend. What do you think you gained from today's workshop?*

Angela: I gained a feeling of love and respect for other women—other Goddesses. I broke down a little bit of my barriers of talking about sex and my sexual experiences. I heard the word masturbation without breaking out in a cold sweat. I had the ability to express myself physically in dance and verbally in words. Thank you, Goddesses, for the experience. I also gained a wonderful foot massage.

God: *Yes, Angela. That was divine. As you can see, there are always lessons in every experience, if you look for them. All of your life has lessons; all of your life is a gift; all of your life holds blessings. Look for the lessons, the gift, the blessings in all aspects of your life, and you will gain spiritually, mentally, and physically from all aspects of your life.*

We can talk again tomorrow. Tomorrow we can talk about sex.

So it was with great interest and a little apprehension that Angela approached her conversation with God the next evening.

Sex

God: *Angela, you know that sex is not normally something people talk about. They like to do it but feel inhibited when talking about it. This leads to many problems throughout society.*

Firstly, between couples. If you don't talk about sex, and what you want out of sex, you are not likely to get it. This leads to people being dissatisfied with their sex lives. Dissatisfaction with a couple's sex life can lead to dissatisfaction in other areas, and couples have broken up over this.

It is much better to bring sex out into the open. Discuss it openly. Discuss your likes and dislikes. Discuss the way you want to be touched, and how you like foreplay, and afterplay. Tell of your wants and desires, your fantasies. Be open about sex, and that can lead to being open about other things in a relationship.

You have already learned that it is desirable to love yourself first, before loving another. This applies to sex as well. You know that once you feel your own love, you can't help but want to share it. It is much easier to share your love if you have given yourself love first. In fact, unless you can feel your own love, it is not possible to give it to another. That's the way it works. Love yourself, then love another.

This inability to talk about sex has a detrimental effect outside of the bedroom as well. You know that rape is not an expression of loving another, but the perpetrators see it as a way of taking love for themselves. It doesn't work, however, for they can't experience love taken by force. It doesn't work that way. So they continue to search for it as serial rapists. They continually try to experience the love that they fail to experience with each rape.

Angela: So what is the answer to this, God?

God: *Your society needs to be more open about sex. Sex education is already taught in many schools, but often it is still not discussed at home. If it is discussed, it is often done in a very clinical way, without much reference to the giving and receiving of love that sex is designed to be.*

Sex can be wonderful. As you learned, sex is always love, but love could be experienced much more joyfully if people lose their inhibitions about discussing sex and enjoying their bodies.

You have beautiful bodies, which can give and receive love with pleasure and joy. Have fun with it. Lighten up with it. Have a romp. Enjoy your own bodies. Enjoy each other's bodies. Make sex the celebration of life, the celebration of love it was meant to be.

Angela: But what of safe sex and contraception, God?

God: *Yes, Angela, these things do need to be considered in the society you now have. In a future society, in which you are more conscious of the law of attraction and your creative abilities, this will not be so much of a concern. But safe sex can still be fun sex.*

Angela, I wanted to talk about sex to you, so you can include it in your book. Start discussing it. It may be embarrassing at first, but the next time you talk about it, it will be less so. As you discovered at your workshop, the more people talk about sex, the more people talk about sex. In other words, one person sees another has been brave enough to do it, and then they feel brave enough to do it.

Perhaps in your New Spirituality study group, you could have a short discussion about your sex lives. Open up to each other. If you can open up to a relative stranger, how easy will it be to discuss your wants and desires with your partner?

Angela: God, I think it would be very hard for most people to talk to virtual strangers about their sex lives, as I found out yesterday. The few words that were spoken caused a fair bit of embarrassment.

God: *But it does get easier, Angela, each time.*

Angela: This is very personal stuff that people would be laying out for all to hear. It would cause people to feel exposed.

God: *Yes, Angela, but if you are aiming for a society where everyone can live in peace, harmony, and love, you know that you have to start seeing others as part of the all that you are—we are all one. This open discussion of sex would be a first small brave step towards that society.*

Angela: That sounds like a big brave step to me.

God: *Take it in small steps, Angela, small brave steps.*

Angela: God, this conversation has not left me feeling the joy I normally feel after talking to you.

God: *No, Angela. It is fear that you are feeling—fear of that exposure that you were talking about.*

Angela: How can I overcome that fear, God?

God: *With love, Angela. The answer to all questions is love. Remember "What would love do now?" Love will see you through any difficulties, including this one. Remember that you have help, and remember that you will never be asked to do more than you can do. Have faith, have love, and all will be well.*

Now, Angela, what I wanted to talk about was not sex, but love, but as you know, sex is the physical form of love. Sex is love-ly. Sex is love, and when you have sex, you are experiencing physical love. Angela, when you are having sex, it is impossible for you to be thinking of fears, or to be angry with others. Sex allows you to love yourself and your partner at the same time. While you are loving yourself and your partner, it is impossible to be thinking fearful thoughts about another. In the New Spirituality, sex will be seen for what it is, not only a wonderful way to love yourself and your partner, but a way to love the world, as well. For, if you are acting with love and thinking love, you are attracting more love to the world. If you think love for the world while you are having sex, and send your love out to all the people, all the creatures of the Earth, and the wonderful Earth herself, you can attract back to you ten times the love you send out. Sex can be the most joyful event of your life, all the while you are loving the world.

I encourage everyone to have more joyful, loving sex, and while having sex, to think love for all the world. If you don't have a partner at this time, you can love yourself. If you do this in a high vibrational state, and also love the world at the same time, you can have orgasm after orgasm, just as you could if you had a partner. Think love, be love, and act with love in all that you do, including sex, and you will be saving the world as you bring yourself and your partner to joyful ecstasy.

Birth Control

God: *Now that everyone knows that sex will save the world, they will be going at it like rabbits, but that might bring up the subject of birth control. You know that rabbits have a lot of babies. In their natural habitat, they have natural predators that keep the population in balance. If they are not in their natural habitat, they just multiply and multiply. They deplete their food stocks until none are left for any other creatures, and they can cause starvation across a number of species, including their own.*

If humans breed without any birth control when they too are having sex like rabbits, they too will have a population that is out of balance. This is what has already happened in some places. There was a very good reason to have big families in olden times: often children died young; you could not be sure you would have a big enough family to carry on the family name, and to see you were looked after into your old age. These days, however, most people can feel quite confident that their children will outlive them and there is no need to have a big family.

As we move into the times of the New Spirituality, everyone will see this, and will want to use birth control, which will become more readily available as religions become more open to the view that sex can be a joy, not just a procreation tool. As we move further into the New

Spirituality, everyone will have greater control of their bodies, using the power of their minds, so birth control will become a thing of the past, as people create the family size they desire, just as they create the rest of their reality.

How Many Partners?

God: *Joy will be available to all, not just those with a partner. Sex and loving yourself physically will be seen as the natural thing it is. It won't be seen as just a procreation tool, but a way to create a joyful life on Earth. Sex will be another way people in the New Spirituality love each other.*

You know from our discussions about Islam that sex between one man and one woman in a monogamous relationship, which grows and develops as you grow and develop, is the easiest way to have a happy, joyful life. But in the days of the New Spirituality, sex between a number of different partners will not be as taboo as it is today. People and religions will be more allowing. They will understand that people have to make their own decisions about how to create the reality they desire. In order to create a reality of a joyful monogamous relationship, they may first want to experience physical love in all its forms with a number of different partners. People in the New Spirituality will know that those who choose to do that are creating the reality they desire, and they will realise that what others choose to do, the reality others choose to create, cannot affect them unless they allow it to.

A Balanced View of Sex

God: *Angela, in the New Spirituality, all will be well. Sex will be seen as the joyful expression of physical love which it was meant to be. It will be more openly discussed, and more openly practised. Because parents will be more open and more loving in front of their children, and children will not think of sex as anything unusual, as anything other than a natural act, children will not be so traumatised as they would today if they saw a couple, or even their parents, having sex. They will learn from a young age that sex is a natural thing. They will be shown that even the birds and the bees do it, even the dragonflies do it, as you saw earlier. Children will not have the issue with sex that they do today, because they will have learned from their parents that it is nothing to be concerned about, but can be a joyful way to love another physically, a way to bring out the joy in another, as they bring out the joy in themselves. Yes, children will want to experiment with their bodies and with other children's bodies, just as they do now, but, whereas now, parents and teachers stop them, in the days of the New Spirituality, they will instruct them instead. They will instruct them on all the aspects of sexuality they need to know to make informed decisions about how they can create the reality they desire.*

In the days of the New Spirituality, everyone will have a balanced view about sex. Although it will be seen as a way to experience and express joyful love, it will not be high on everyone's priority list as it is today, because it won't be on everyone's minds. You know that you attract what you think about, and in times to come, sex will not be a big issue, so people will not attract more and more thoughts about it. People will understand this, so if they wish to have a life that has a strong sexual focus, they will understand that they merely have to think about sex a lot, and sex will come to them. However, if they wish to focus on other things, and sexual thoughts do occur, they will understand that they merely need to not give it another thought.

Angela, sex will be a joy for all. It will no longer be seen as something dirty, but as a joyful experience of love, a joyful experience of another of God's gifts. As we move into the New Spirituality, sex will be seen as another way to experience each other as children of God. For God so loved the world that God created in each being a way to experience divine union with another of its species. In experiencing this divine union, you can experience the divine in each other and in yourselves.

Love is the Answer

God: *Angela, I wanted to talk to you about love. I love you; you know that, and I love all of my creation. For I am love, and so are you, and all of my creation is love. But Angela, love is not just what we are; it is what we can use to bring about the New Spirituality. You know that thinking love allows you to enjoy your day more. It allows you to be more tolerant of others' faults, and your faults. Thinking love will allow you to be closer to your true loving self. If you can think love towards others, you are encouraging them to see themselves as they really are, which is pure love. The more love in your thoughts, the more love in your life and in others' lives. This is where that snowball comes in. Your snowball of love, which starts with your thoughts of love, can lead to others having thoughts of love, which can lead yet others to having thoughts of love. Your love, which starts in your thoughts, can take over the world.*

The more you think love, it isn't just making you have a better day; it is saving the world.

Islam

After starting her New Spirituality study group, Angela's interest in all religions was revitalised. She found it a joy to learn about the positive aspects of the different religions, and an even greater joy to learn what she believed to be God's point of view on their beliefs, at least in the beginning.

The Koran

God: *Angela, I wanted to talk to you about the documentary you watched last night about the Koran[24]. The program gave a fairly balanced view of The Koran, and its key elements. As you learned in your study of the Christian Bible, there are many discrepancies. The same applies to the Koran.*

You know, Angela, that God would not demand the harsh punishments mentioned in that documentary like cutting off hands, etc.. God would never condone beating one's wife, no matter how she behaved.

As you learned in the Conversations With God *books, God does not care what you do, except that God loves you, and wants the best for all of you. It's up to each one of you to decide what that best is. It is not God's wish to impose*

God's will on anyone, as we have discussed before. If you feel that those harsh punishments are what is best for you, then carry on doing it. But don't do it in the name of God. For God is all love. You are all love.

God would suggest that what is best for all people and creatures of the Earth would be to recognise what you are, which is all love, and to find the best way to be that.

Love would not do many of those things discussed on your documentary, Angela. Love would consider the good of the all, including those who had done the so-called 'wrong'. Love would never inflict mutilation of female genitalia, as was described in your documentary as female circumcision. Love would not inflict mutilation of male genitalia, either, for that matter.

Angela: God, I have come to understand that we are all love, and I agree with all you have said here. I just want to be certain that I have recorded your words accurately, and not biased them in any way.

God: *Angela, you know that you have been practising with Jesus recording our messages word for word, and letter for letter. You know that if there is an error, I will tell you. These words are mine, but as in all messages, they are filtered through your mind, so you know that the words are mine, but perhaps the tone is yours.*

Angela: Is there anything you want to add, then, God.

God: *No, Angela. The message is very clear: stop committing atrocities in the name of God or Allah. As we have discussed before, if you want to know the best course of action in any situation, ask: "What would love do now?" and your first answer is always the right one.*

Angela: If Muslims want to change their religion, they might have to accept that the Koran is not 100% the word of God.

God: *As you saw in the documentary, Angela, there are many discrepancies caused by the original recordings of the Koran without the dots. More work will be done on finding the true word of God within this sacred text.*

The documentary Angela had watched, had explained that a very early version of the Koran was discovered, in which the dots were missing from the text. Apparently, at the time of the prophet Muhammad, everyone spoke Syrio-Aramaic, and at the time that the texts were written in Arabic, it was a new language. The pages that were found apparently show some alteration to the texts.

The documentary also described the differences between the Shia and Sunni sects, as similar to the differences between Protestants and Catholics.

God: *Muslims, as well as people of other faiths, can know that the Word of God is not in a book, but in their hearts. God lives now within each and every one of you. When you inflict harsh punishment on another, you inflict harsh punishment on God, and ultimately on yourself, for we are all one.*

Angela, I don't want to give your readers the impression that the Koran is any more flawed than any other sacred text. It may, in fact, be less so. What I do want to impress upon your readers is that, whilst you can learn much from all these sacred texts, the key to finding God, and finding God within you, is to go within. Look for God everywhere, but find God within yourself first. Once you find God within yourself, you will notice that God is in all people, in all things.

Reconciliation

God: *Angela, I wanted to talk to you about the book you have started to read—*Reconciliation[25] *by Benazir Bhutto. You have already begun to feel a certain affinity with this woman, after reading just one chapter. You know that she gave her life to bring these words to the world, and in an attempt to bring reconciliation to the world, and to her people—the Muslim community in general, and the Pakistani people in particular.*

You can be a voice for reconciliation as well, Angela. You can embrace the message that she has delivered to you and the world. Think love in all that you do, and you cannot fail. Take Benazir's message of reconciliation, and add your love to her love, to others of her kind's love, and spread that love, that reconciliation throughout the world.

You can do that with this book, with your visits, your thoughts, your actions, and your words. Your love can bring peace to the world, Angela.

You have learned the power of your thoughts, your affirmations, during your week of skiing. Imagine what you can do with your thoughts when millions of others are adding their thoughts of peace to yours. Go now and be a voice for peace wherever you go. Be my confident, faithful, invincible, beacon of love to the world.

Angela had only taken up skiing later in life, and was not at all confident in her abilities, but as God said, she found that during her recent trip her positive thoughts and affirmations had definitely helped her confidence, which led to her improving her skills.

After she completed reading the book, Angela spoke to God again.

Angela: I wanted to talk about what I read in *Reconciliation*, where Benazir reminded me that Muslims consider Muhammad to be the last prophet—the last person to have heard the word of God. I would think this would be a big obstacle to overcome if the New Spirituality is to influence Muslim countries, because they would not believe that these conversations have been with God, if God hasn't spoken to anyone since Muhammad.

God: *Yes, Angela. This will be an obstacle, but as with all things, love will overcome this obstacle as well. All will be revealed to you as you require it, but know that love will conquer any difficulties and overcome any problems. Your love, my love, and the love of all those who seek peace in the world can combine to overcome any differences which may separate you.*

You know that there are many belief systems in the world, but just because two people or two million people believe different things, it doesn't mean that they can't all live in peace and harmony together. Just because two people or two million people have different belief systems, it doesn't mean that each one of those people has nothing to say which would be of benefit to you, of relevance to you, of interest to you. As I mentioned when we discussed your New Spirituality study group, there is much to learn from all religions, and from all people of the world. Just because Muslims have a different belief system to you, it doesn't mean that they will discard all that you have to say. Many within the Muslim community understand the significance, the necessity for diversity of beliefs in the world.

As you learned from The Vortex[26] *by Jerry & Esther Hicks & Abraham, without the diversity that exists in the world, there would not be any evolution; there would be nothing for each person to choose from, and therefore move the universe forward with new ideas and new ways of looking at life. Angela, many in the Muslim community will value your commitment to peace and love, even if they don't accept the origin of these messages.*

Democracy

God: *Angela, you have read how the West has thwarted democracy in many countries of the world. You already knew that governments of certain Western countries manipulated activities in a number of countries to bring about certain ends. They have used the philosophy that the ends justified the means, and quite often the ends they achieved were not what they hoped for, and often weren't what they told the people of their countries. Even though those countries have caused difficulties in a number of countries, that is no reason for people of those oppressed countries to hold a grudge against the people of the oppressing countries, who were usually unaware of the covert activities of their government.*

Angela: In a democracy, it is probably beholden of a people to know what their government is up to, but, I, for one, have not always taken an interest in our government's activities. I guess there are many others like me.

God: *That's right, Angela. Once you have elected a government, whether of your choice or not, it is quite often the people's attitude that they have done their bit, and can leave all the details up to their government.*

Angela: A functioning media would seem vital, God.

God: *Yes, Angela.*

Angela: Quite often our media tends to pick on governments for what seem like insignificant details, and probably let more significant problems go unreported.

God: *That may be the case, Angela, but the media are working on supply and demand, as with any product.*

Angela: I guess.

God: *Anyway, Angela, you can point out that what has happened with Western governments in the past is certainly no indication of the will of the people those governments represent, in the present, or the future.*

Angela: This may be a good time to ask a question I had been saving for Abraham, if I ever went to one of the Abraham-Hicks seminars. There is a suggestion by Abraham that it would serve us best to be more allowing, which I take to mean that you allow others to live the lives they choose, and that need not affect the life I, myself, choose. This would seem to lead to a tendency for fewer rules and regulations. However, it would seem to me that people who are more allowing may be less likely to want to become a part of a government which tries to control how people live. My question is: Does this mean that we are destined to be ruled by people who are not allowing, because they are the only ones who run for government?

God: *Well, Angela, that is a good question. As with all things, you are the creator of your own reality, along with those around you. If you and those around you will an allowing government, then the universe must deliver. The universe will find some among you who wish to be the cause of your government becoming more allowing. These people will be able to put in place measures which lead your country, and your world, if you so wish, into an atmosphere of allowing.*

Angela: OK God. Sounds good.

God: *Here again, Angela, love is the key. You know that many rules and regulations have been put in place to protect people from something they fear. Love can conquer all of these fears, thus removing the need for protection from them.*

It had been many weeks since she last spoke to God in a formal way, but after Angela finished reading the Koran[27] for her New Spirituality study group, she was keen to learn what God had to say about its teachings.

Angela: It's been a while, God.

God: *Yes, Angela, but remember: it's easier than riding a bicycle.*

Angela: God, you know that our meeting today is very important for both of us, so I am particularly anxious to get it right.

God: *I know, Angela. Have faith and all will be well.*

Angela: I have complete faith in you, and faith in my abilities is as good as it can be considering my human frailties.

God: *That's good, Angela. Shall we commence?*

Hell

Angela: OK, God. Number one on my list of discussion points is the big thing in the Koran—hell, hellfire, eternal flames for those unbelievers, and others who cause you wrath.

God: *You are right; this is a big one. You know you read in the Dummies book [*The Koran for Dummies[28] *by Sohaib Sultan] that the carrot of paradise for those who do good works, required a stick for those who do evil. As you know, the Koran was written in a different time. At that time there was great evil. I know you think of the times now as embodying much evil, but in the time of Muhammad, it was necessary to give people a look at the other side of the coin. You know that what goes around comes around, and that there are consequences for all evil* *practices, as well as for good practices, but it was not really possible in the culture of Muhammad to point out that every action has an equal and opposite reaction. That concept is easy for people to grasp today, because of their knowledge of the laws of physics, but in Muhammad's time, it was necessary to offer them some knowledge that they would be rewarded according to their actions, both good and evil.*

Angela: But is unbelieving evil, God? Will that be rewarded with evil?

God: *Not per se, Angela. But unbelievers are more easily led into temptation, and more easily left to resort to evil, as they don't have the connection with God which keeps them on the straight path.*

Angela: The Koran does state that people will be "rewarded for their deeds"[i], so I guess that all fits.

Number two continues on from number one: the Koran confirms a number of times that we must believe in the earlier prophets and the Torah. Those stories include a lot of scourges and smiting of people. Is that just more of the same?

God: *Yes, Angela. As was mentioned in the Koran, not all of the words of the Torah, or the Christian Gospels have*

---

[i] 34:38

been kept in their original form, but the idea behind smiting and the scourges is the same—to make people realise that evil actions will have evil consequences.

Angela: Is this the same reason that God states in the Koran "Fear me"?

God: *Yes and no, Angela. Yes, it is meant to make people consider the consequences of their actions, but the Arabic words have a slightly different meaning—more of an idea of submission.*

Consequences

Angela: "Say: 'Unbelievers...You have your religion, and I have mine'"[i]. "Bear with them and wish them peace"[ii]. "Bear patiently with what they say and leave their company without recrimination"[iii].

God, the Koran seems to be promoting tolerance and yet in other parts, it states that God will not forgive those that serve other Gods, that it is a heinous sin, and that God will not forgive idolatry. I thought you didn't believe in sin.

God: *No, Angela, sin is not something that affects me, and as per our discussions about the friendly soul, there really*

---

[i] 109:1
[ii] 43:89
[iii] 73:11

is no Satan. There are agreements among souls to be a 'victim' or a 'perpetrator' in certain circumstances, but there are still consequences to all of those actions, whether or not there has been an agreement.

Angela: God, if I kill someone in this life, and then I agree to be their victim in the next life, they wouldn't have to pay for that sin in terms of consequences, would they?

God: *Yes, Angela. Every action has a consequence, even if there are no victims.*

Angela: This is why the Koran suggests we "requite evil with good"[i], to break the cycle?

God: *That's right, Angela. Well done. As we discussed before, love will prevail in any circumstances, so the best way to break the cycle of 'evil' is to respond to every circumstance with love.*

Idolatry

Angela: God, what about idolatry? Why is that heinous?

God: *Well, Angela, if someone is concentrating all of their*

---

[i] 23:93, see also 28:53

efforts on worshipping idols, they are not forming a close association with the one true God who dwells within them.

Angela: And you can't forgive them?

God: *As we discussed before, Angela, God cannot forgive any sin, because God does not see any action as a sin, but at the time of Muhammad, that was a concept that could easily be understood.*

Angela: In another part of the Koran, it states that God forgives all sins, but I guess the poor idolaters missed out.

God: *Yes, Angela. There is a reason for this as well. As you know, God doesn't forgive, but allows you to forgive yourself. If you develop a connection to God, you can, indeed, come to a place where you can forgive yourself for the most heinous of sin. But without that connection to God, you cannot reach that level of forgiveness for yourself. Those who worship false gods cannot reach that connection, because they are barking up the wrong tree, so to speak. To a lesser extent, unbelievers come into the same category. Although it is possible to form a connection with God without believing in God (for we are all connected— I am as close as your jugular[i], as you know), it is much easier to form a strong bond, a close connection if you believe in me.*

---

[i] 50:15

Sacred rites

Angela: Sacred rites is next, God. In *Tomorrow's God*[29], you said you didn't require worship, and yet you are asking people to submit to you, and then asking them to do all sorts of rites in order to worship you: fasting and pilgrimage, both with strict rules about what you should do and when, and prayer five times a day after first going through elaborate cleansing.

God: *Yes, Angela, this does sound unlike the God you met in* Tomorrow's God, *and the God you have come to know, but what if I told you that God does not require any of these things for God, but all of these rites are in order to benefit those who practise them?*

Angela: Well, the first question that comes to mind is: what benefit is washing your feet, washing your arms to the elbow, and snorting up water?

God: *Well, Angela, it is impossible to think of mundane things while you are snorting up water, as you put it. All of these rites have a benefit for the person performing them.*

Angela: One reason given for fasting is to "magnify God"[i], and give thanks for guidance.

God: *That's right, Angela. For if you magnify God, your*

---

[i] 2:186

focus on God increases, and therefore it is easier to stay connected to God, and as you have become aware, what you are grateful for in advance becomes part of your reality. Giving thanks for guidance you have received in the form of the Koran allows more guidance to come into your reality.

Worship of God

Angela: "All who dwell in the heavens and on the earth shall prostrate themselves before God: some willingly, some perforce"[i]. I thought you didn't require worship.

God: *No, Angela, I don't, and I have to say that this passage is a little bit of poetic license, in that, this passage was comparing the effects the idols could have compared to the effect the one true God could have. As Jesus pointed out, he, like many in the spiritual and physical realms, are happy to see God's will be done, so this is a form of prostration.*

Prayer

Angela: "Recite your prayers at sunset, at nightfall, and at dawn… Pray during the night as well"[ii].

God: *Angela, prayer is what brings the practitioner closer*

---

[i] 13:15   [ii] 17:79

to God. The more times it can be done, the more often they will feel close to God. You have discovered a way to be close to God without formal prayer, but formal prayer is a way for those who have no other means of accessing that connection, to connect to God regularly.

Cleanliness

Angela: The next one I find difficult to comprehend, God. "purify your garments and keep away from uncleanness"[i]. "God loves those that…strive to keep themselves clean"[ii]. We already heard how you want people to wash before prayer. What's this big hangup of yours about being clean? I thought I had an obsession about cleanliness.

God: *You do, Angela. Mine is not an obsession. In asking people to strive to keep clean, I am asking them to keep their entire being clean—body, mind and spirit. It is much easier to have a clean spirit if you have a clean mind; it is much easier to have a clean mind if you have a clean body, and if you have a clean body, mind and spirit, it is much easier to stay connected to God.*

Angela: "Do not approach your prayers…when you are unclean"[iii].

---

[i] 74:1
[ii] 2:222
[iii] 4:43

God: Yes, Angela, we covered the reasons for washing before prayer very briefly. It is a way to prepare your mind for prayer. It has little to do with the state of the body.

Angela: "Believers,…idolaters are unclean. Let them not approach the Sacred Mosque"[i].

God: *Yes, Angela. As you know, from your recent experiences with auras, and from your lessons about surrounding yourself in white light, it is quite easy to take on negative aspects into your aura, into your energy field. Idolaters are more likely to have a contaminated energy field, which can then bring negative energy into the sacred mosque. It was therefore suggested that they be kept away, so as not to contaminate those "clean" worshippers. You know that it is easier to keep your energy field clean than it is to clean it once it is contaminated.*

Submission

Angela: When thinking about your earlier answer about submission, I thought I should mention our conversation the other day, God. You said that all of the rites were developed to benefit the practitioner, and another day we might talk about those in more depth, but people may wonder why you require submission.

---

[i] 9:28

Should I tell them about my experience with submission?

God: *Yes, Angela, please do.*

Angela: Well, from memory, I was asking for my leg to be healed (after a knee injury which left me somewhat debilitated), and you said if I would allow it, you would like to allow things to take place according to your divine plan, which would have added benefit. I submitted to your will, and as well as seeing that added benefit come about—which was Bill becoming much more accepting of my beliefs—I discovered an unforeseen benefit in submission itself. I discovered that I felt so much closer to you, since submitting to your will. When I asked you, you said that when my ego got out of the way, I was allowed a closer connection with you. You said I still need my ego to get along in the world, but when it took a back seat, I felt closer to you. Does that sound about right, God?

God: *Yes, Angela. Pretty close.*

God's Will

Angela: God, regarding submitting to your will, I am a little confused about how that works. Can I just leave everything up to you now? I don't have to give these things another thought?

God: *No, Angela. Once you have asked for something and submitted to my will—my divine plan—you can, indeed, forget about it, unless of course you can't. As you know, Angela, others' wills come into play in many things you request, so it is good to keep some positive thoughts, actions, and affirmations regarding your desire. That way the universe is reminded of your will. Quite often, if there are two opposing thoughts regarding a desire, the person who has had the most focus succeeds.*

Angela: But God, I thought the universe had to find a way to bring everyone their desires?

God: *It does, Angela, but it could take a while, if it has to ensure other more dominant opposing desires are met first.*

Angela: Where does your will come into it?

God: *Angela, my will will be done if you have submitted your desire to my will, only providing it does not impede on any other being's free will. As we discussed before, free will is paramount.*

Angela: So people who believe that nothing happens unless it is God's will are mistaken?

God: *Yes and no, Angela. They are right that nothing can happen unless I allow it to happen, but has everything happened the way I would have preferred? Definitely not!*

But having said that, the outcome of every action has a positive effect for all souls involved, but sometimes only in a spiritual sense.

Covering Up

Angela: The next one is a big one for me, God. It is about chastity, about not displaying women's "adornments"[i]; "Good women…guard their unseen parts because God has guarded them"[ii]; asks women "to draw their veils over their bosoms"[iii]. God, I got the impression that you were happier with free love, that we shouldn't be ashamed of our bodies. Yet the Koran states that Satan revealed Adam's and Eve's "shameful parts"[iv]. How can we celebrate our bodies and feel open about discussing sex, when we have to think of our genitals as shameful parts, and have to cover all of our bodies if we are women?

God: *Angela, as you suspected, the covering of the female body is very much a cultural thing. The idea of covering bosoms was meant to stop women in Muhammad's day from becoming victims of violence against them, which was rife in that day, in that age; whereas on a nudist beach today, there is unlikely to be any attacks on women because most men are there to get some sun, not some sex. But having said that, until*

---

[i] 24:31
[ii] 4:34
[iii] 24:31
[iv] 7:25

love becomes the predominant force in people's lives, there is still a risk of inciting some men to lustful thoughts or actions if they are given too much temptation.

As fashions change, temptation is more likely to be encountered if men see parts of a woman they are unused to seeing, so for an interpretation of this part which reads "except such as are normally revealed"[i], it is best to change fashion slowly to allow more flesh to be revealed, if that is your desire. But if all men embrace love, they will not be tempted by the show of flesh of any kind.

As we discovered during our discussions about highly evolved beings, they are not so focused on sex, and see it as a natural part of life and love. They would no more take advantage of a woman who exposed her genitals, than they would a woman who covered herself from head to toe. But in order to get to that stage of development, humans need to embrace love in all its forms and lose their hang-ups about sex. I suggest regular discussions between spouses and with others in the community about sex to help build a world where women are safer to walk the streets in whatever attire they desire, without fear of being accosted or assaulted.

Angela: God, why call them our shameful parts?

God: *You may find, Angela, that this is another connotation which comes from a mistranslation of the*

---

[i] 24:31

original Arabic or Syrio-Aramaic, as the original Arabic tongue was then spoken. I believe the original words had a meaning closer to private, unseen parts.

Angela: "And when they had eaten of the tree, their shame became visible to them"[i]. Is this shame that became visible to them another mistranslation?

God: *Yes, Angela, but this is closer to correct. The Arabic words do contain an element of shame, but the emphasis is more on unseen. In other words, Adam and Eve saw themselves in a whole new light after partaking of the tree.*

Angela: So the story of Adam and Eve is a true story, not a parable or something?

God: *Remember, Angela, when we discussed creation, and I said that it didn't have to be a choice between evolution and the six days of creation, that it could be both/and. Well, the same applies to the story of Adam and Eve.*

Spouses

Angela: You "created...spouses" to "live in peace with them" and "planted love and kindness"[ii] in our hearts. This sounds a bit more like my God.

---

[i] 7:20

[ii] 30:19

God: *Yes Angela. Your God loves you, and wants you all to be happy and live in peace, if that is your desire.*

Chastity

Angela: God, there is a long list of actions and attributes that the Koran states God wants of us. A few have caused questions, which seem to come back to sex again—to be chaste and to avoid lewd acts. Why do we need to be chaste and avoid lewd acts?

God: *Well, Angela, chastity is in the eye of the beholder. A person who has had no sexual partners is chaste to everyone, but those who have had only a few are relatively chaste to those who have had lots. But the reason for enjoining chastity is to allow husbands and wives to discover the intricacy of each other's bodies together for the first time. There is no greater gift that a woman can give a man, or a man can give a woman, than to allow the other to discover the intricacies of their bodies which no other person has witnessed. As you have found, Angela, from your long relationship with Bill, as your relationship develops, it changes as you change, as you grow up and grow older. You rediscover ways to love each other, as your needs and tastes change. You can make your sexual life a reflection of a growing and changing relationship, as you and your relationship matures. You can support each other with sexual love, as well as emotional love, through the ups and downs of your married life. As with all aspects of the*

Koran, this is a way to enhance people's lives, not a strict rule with punishment of death.

Punishment

Angela: No, God. I think, from memory, the adulterer and adulteress are to be given 100 lashes[i]. While we are on the subject of punishment, you said to me that there is no punishment (by God), and that we shouldn't be acting like a God that we thought promoted punishment. So, why do you give punishments in the Koran?

God: *Angela this, too, needs to be looked at in the context of the times and places in which it is given. At the time the revelation was given, death or worse punishment was given for even the most minor of crimes. I suggested to Muhammad that cutting off the hand of a thief would stop them from reoffending, but that forgiveness is better. You can kill a murderer, but forgiveness is better. One hundred lashes for adultery, but forgiveness is better.*

Angela: But why is adultery a crime?

God: *Angela, you know that it was part of the original covenant between the Israelites and God. Although I suggested that it was not in their best interests to practise*

---

[i] 24:1

adultery, the words were distorted to make it a punishable crime. Instead of punishing adultery by stoning, as was practiced before the Koran, I set down suggestions for reducing the punishment to a flogging, and put in place such strict criteria of proof that make it virtually impossible to prove and convict.

Angela: God, why not get rid of punishment altogether, as you have asked us to do now?

God: *Different times, Angela, require different approaches. The world was not ready then for this snowball of love we are preparing for it now. As we discussed earlier, there was still a requirement for a stick to go with the carrot. Today's times will allow for punishment to become a thing of the past, if enough people embrace love and allow the snowball to build.*

Angela: I was reading today, God, on a newsletter from Amnesty International, about the vote to abolish the death penalty at the United Nations, which had the greatest number of "fors" they have ever had in such a vote.

God: *Yes, Angela, this is one small brave step, or perhaps you could call this a big brave step if it actually leads to that outcome.*

Angela: So, we don't need the stick anymore, God?

God: *No, Angela. Love will prevail always. Think love, be love, and act with love, and you cannot fail.*

More on Chastity

Angela: The Koran states that Muslims can marry slave-girls as long as they are chaste and have not entertained men[i]. God, in today's society, there are not many slave-girls, but there are a lot of unchaste girls, who have entertained men. So, they are not really good enough?

God: *Angela, this is a complex issue. As we discussed earlier, God suggested chastity as a way to allow men and women to give each other their bodies as gifts on their wedding night. But also, as we said before, chastity is a relative thing. One particular reason for suggesting Muslims only marry those who are chaste is that they then have no worries about sexually transmitted diseases.*

Angela: But God, it seems to be only asking Muslim women to be chaste—slave-girls, and not the men.

God: *If a man is already chaste, he cannot spread disease to a chaste woman. In the days of Muhammad, it was common practice to use slave-girls as sex slaves, which may be shared among men. Muslim men were asked to avoid such women. Muslim women had no equivalent type of*

---

[i] 4:25

male to avoid. Muslim men and women were both asked to marry only believing men and women, who would therefore be more chaste, and therefore more free from disease.

Lewdness

Angela: "Satan…enjoins lewdness on you"[i]. What exactly is lewdness, anyway?

God: *My definition, Angela, would be the opposite of chastity. We already discussed the benefits of chastity for newlyweds, but there are other benefits as well. You know that those who flit from one one-night-stand to another are rarely happy. True happiness is much easier to attain in a loving long-term relationship.*

More Punishment

Angela: Women who "commit a lewd act,…confine them to their houses till death overtakes them or till God finds another way for them", and "if two men…commit a lewd act, punish them both" unless they repent, and change their ways, then "let them be"[ii]. For a God who doesn't believe in punishment, you sure have a lot of it in your 'Book'.

---

[i] 2:268   [ii] 4:15-16

God: *Yes, Angela, we discussed the reasons for punishing adultery, which was related to the original covenant from the Torah. Women of Muhammad's day who committed lewd acts were stoned to death, as were men who fornicated together. These punishments, like those previously discussed, were a step forward in those days—a lot of steps actually.*

Angela: But it's not exactly axe-murdering. Why not change your covenant, and say it was only a suggestion; it's just not recommended?

God: *People of that day would not have given up punishment of lewd acts and adultery because they strongly believed that the word of God had said it was a sin.*

Angela: But God, Jews today who are working from the Torah, don't stone adulterers and lewd people, only Muslims, or so-called Muslims, even though your book doesn't give that as a punishment; not in my version, anyway.

God: *No, Angela. Different societies have developed in different ways. Some societies which claim to practise Islam distort the laws of punishment to fit what they believe is correct. Even now, some societies are practising pre-Muhammadan punishment.*

Homosexuality

Angela: In relation to Lot's people, there is the discussion about fornicating with males, which makes them transgressors[i]. So it seems that homosexuality is a sin (even though you don't believe in sin), but God did you not create homosexuals? It seems obvious to me they are born that way and it was not something they chose. So why do you say it's a sin?

God: *Angela, the homosexuals in Lot's day were fornicating with men other than homosexuals. They were corrupting young men, and heterosexual men were leaving their wives to have sex with men, and then returning to their wives without remorse.*

Homosexuality is not a sin, Angela. As you say, they are born that way. However, two males together often do not have the balancing stability which a female's character can bring to a relationship. As with heterosexuals, if homosexuals practise chastity and give each other the gift of each other's bodies, they have nothing to fear. It is only when they seek to denigrate themselves and their bodies by 'quickies' in the lavatories that they will end up with difficulties. As with any so-called sin, the transgression is not really against God, for God has no feelings on the matter, the transgression is on their souls, and perhaps on their society.

---

[i] 26:170

Angela: God, is not a 'quicky' in the lavatory still an act of love?

God: *Yes, sex is an act of love, but a man is not usually even loving himself in that situation, and certainly not the other, whom he has only just met and is merely using as a tool, similar to prostitution. It relates to our discussion about rape. In the case of the 'quicky' in the lavatory, there is rarely any love experienced, even though it is an act of love. Rarely would a man who has love for himself perform such acts, but it is love that he is searching for.*

Angela: You are sounding like a judgmental God.

God: *No, Angela. As with all these things, I merely point out what does and doesn't serve you, given who you are and where you want to go.*

Multiple Wives

Angela: God, you said that it is the greatest gift a husband and wife can give to each other, but if a husband already has a wife or two, or three, it seems a bit of a one-sided gift, and not in keeping with the exchange you mentioned.

God: *That is correct, Angela. When allowing for a number of wives, the Koran is, again, a reflection of its time, but it does state that if you can't give equal attention to all your wives, then you shouldn't take another.*

In view of our discussion about the reasons for chastity, it is not really possible to give the same attention, the same gift of chastity, to a second wife.

Marriage to Non-Believers

Angela: "You shall not wed pagan women, unless they embrace the Faith"[i], but "lawful for you are believing women"[ii]. More laws, God. What's wrong with a bit of contrast in a marriage? My atheist husband is no less a wonderful husband because he lacks faith.

God: *Yes, he is, actually. You know you have wished for, asked for, prayed for his conversion.*

Angela: Yes, but had I been a Muslim woman, I wouldn't be allowed to even try to convert him.

God: *You know these laws are there to make life easier for those who follow Islam.*

Angela: It creates an 'us' and 'them' situation, God. It divides humanity.

God: *You are right, Angela, but that divide would be there regardless. It is much more difficult to connect with*

---

[i] 2:221 [ii] 5:5

those who aren't connected to God. Yes, everyone is connected to God, but many don't realise it. It is much easier to form a loving bond with those who are connected to God.

Angela: There are a lot of atheist couples out there who would argue with you. What of Buddhists, God? They don't normally believe in God, and yet they practise compassion and love. I don't know much about the Pagan religion, but they probably do, as well.

God: *You are right, Angela. All religions have some elements of truth, but if you see a religion as a means to an end—the end being a close association with God—then Islam is the straight path to that end.*

Angela: I would think that the end that people seek in religion would be happiness.

God: *Many are seeking happiness, Angela, and Islam provides that as well.*

Angela: You sound like you're trying to make a sale.

God: *No, Angela. I already have sold you on the benefits of God. I don't need to sell you Islam.*

Domination of Women

Angela: The next one is a big one, God. the Koran states that if your wives are disobedient, you can "beat them", that "men have authority over women", and that you have "made one superior to the other"[i]. "Women are your fields: go, then, into your fields whence you please"[ii]. "Women shall with justice have rights similar to those exercised against them, although men have a status above them"[iii].

I'm sorry, God. I can't listen to any excuses for beating women. I'm having trouble listening here.

God: *I know, Angela. I'm not pleased by this either. This is one of the very few translation errors from the original text. The Arabic word is slightly different, but has a great difference in meaning. The original word means something like admonish.*

Angela: But why do we need admonishing? Why must we be obedient to men? Is that because you have created men to be superior to women?

God: *Quite the opposite, Angela. A man needs the guiding hand of a woman, who is indeed superior to a man in many ways. There can only be one leader in any pack, and even though I suggest that decisions should be made by consensus,*

---

[i] 4:34
[ii] 2:223
[iii] 2:228

when there is no consensus, the man's decision should be accepted. As a woman has many wiles, she is in a better position to see her decision accepted by her husband. This is one way she is made superior. Another is her ability to humbly accept her husband's wishes, when the issue is not something she feels strongly about. She is more likely to be able to see the bigger picture, and realise that what she loses on the roundabouts she gains on the swings.

Angela: And what about being men's fields, and they can enter us whence they please?

God: *Angela, just as a man needs to work hard at his fields, he also needs to work hard at keeping his wife happy. Just as an untended field is unlikely to produce a crop, so an untended wife is unlikely to satisfy her husband's desires.*

But the other meaning does apply as well. Both men and women should rejoice in their bodies, and celebrate them together as husband and wife whenever they desire. As we discussed before, Angela, sex is a wonderful thing, and should be celebrated as and when it is desired.

Angela: But don't the fields get a say?

God: *Yes, of course. Without consent, sex is not love, but rape. As we discussed before, without a consenting partner, the perpetrator cannot experience love.*

Angela: And what about men's status over women when it comes to rights?

God: *This status was put in place to allow men to be financially responsible for women, as men were usually the breadwinners. As can be seen with Muhammad's example with his first wife, women can be affluent and be career oriented. It is quite reasonable that other arrangements could be made to allow a woman's money to be used to support the family, but remember that the Koran was revealed at a time when women had no rights at all.*

Here, again, consensus is best, so as not to place too heavy a responsibility on a man who may want to be a stay-at-home dad while a wife works, or on a woman who may want to have a career and a family. But, as you have seen recently in your own family, trying to maintain a career and be a mother can take its toll on women. The laws relating to women in Islam were set up with this in mind.

Angela: This seems to be a big divide between Western and Muslim women. It is the view of many Western women that their Muslim counterparts are treated as second-class citizens, are confined to their home, and treated as baby-making machines, and I think it is the view of many women in Muslim countries that Western women are worked to the bone as they try to maintain a career and raise a family, and in the end fail at both.

God: *Well, Angela, unfortunately there is some truth to both of those stereotypes. But there are many on both sides who are happy in their roles, and those stereotypes are extremes of both lifestyles.*

Angela: It would seem that the birth rate in Muslim countries would support that stereotype.

God: *Perhaps, Angela, but if you start to get to know some Muslim women, you might be surprised.*

War

Angela: God, the next question is about war. "Fight for the cause of God"[i]; "fight with…wealth and…persons in the cause of God"[ii]; "slay the idolaters wherever you find them"[iii]; "Idolatry is more grievous than bloodshed"[iv]; "Fight against them until idolatry is no more and God's religion reigns supreme"[v].

God: *Angela, these are more of those passages which need to be looked at in light of the era of the revelation. If Muhammad and his followers had not been prepared to make war, the world would now be a very sorry place.*

---

[i] various
[ii] 49:15
[iii] 9:5
[iv] 2:190
[v] 2:193

Angela: It seems it is a sorry place, God, and one of the reasons for this seems to be that some people are still fighting in what they see as the cause of God.

God: *You are right, Angela.*

Angela: So what do we do about it?

God: *Love, Angela, is the answer to all questions. Love would tell you that the reason people feel a need to fight in the cause of God is firstly they have lost their connection to God. Praying for them and sending them love will help. Secondly, discourse with them would allow them to air their grievances. Perhaps they have valid grievances which can be addressed, without resorting to any fighting. But no matter what the cause of their attitude, love is the key to finding a solution.*

Angela: "The words of God shall never change"[i]. The Koran gives the impression that you can strike off the heads of the unbelievers on the battlefield, wherever it may be, and these words remain valid, along with all of your punishment laws, forever and ever.

God: *Yes, Angela, if taken out of context you could say that. But you have to look at the context of the fighting that was enjoined in the Koran. You also have to look at*

---

[i] 10:65

the context of God in the Koran. God is compassionate and merciful. Emulate him.

Angela: "Retaliation is decreed for you in bloodshed"[i].

God: *Yes, Angela, that passage also talks about a slave for a slave, as well as if there is a pardon. Just as slavery has nearly become a thing of the past so too retaliation can be, if one follows God's path of compassion and mercy.*

Angela: "Let those who would exchange the life of this world for the Hereafter, fight for the cause of God"[ii]. It also talks about those who give away their lives in order to find favour with God. You can understand why some think suicide bombing is OK.

God: *Yes, Angela, they have taken those passages out of context, just as you have. Can one find justification for killing in the Koran? Yes. Is that following the path of God? No. God is compassionate and merciful.*

Acts of Terror

Angela: "He guides the hearts of those who believe in Him"[iii]. God, what about those who profess to believe

---

[i] 2:178
[ii] 4:74
[iii] 64:11

in you, but fly planes into buildings, or blow up innocent people. Do you guide their hearts too?

God: *You know the answer to that, Angela. No one who commits such acts can have the slightest connection to God, for God would lead them in a totally different direction. Those whose hearts are guided by God foster love wherever they go. They would never harm the life of a non-combatant, and they would not tolerate 'collateral damage'.*

More Killing

Angela: God, there are a number of passages regarding war and fighting for the cause of God which still trouble me. I know you said that the fight is over, and it only related to Muhammad's time, but would you like to comment on the following:

"When you meet the unbelievers in the battlefield strike off their heads"[i] and "do not…sue for peace when you have gained the upper hand"[ii].

God: *Angela, as we discussed earlier, that is only in relation to the battles which Muhammad conducted. I know the image of striking off heads is not a pleasant one, but any war is bloody, and this was no different. As for not suing for peace, that was relating to one particular foe at*

---

[i] 47:4 [ii] 47:35

one particular time—a foe who could not be trusted to uphold any treaty. You know that in other areas of the Koran there is a suggestion that if they incline to peace, make peace with them, which was the suggestion for other battles that Muhammad fought.

But Angela, you should not let those short passages about war deflect you from the real message of the Koran— the message that God is compassionate and merciful, and you can be too.

Angela: I will try, God.

Animal Welfare

Angela: According to The Koran, you have subjected the beasts to men for riding and eating[i].

God: *Yes, Angela. You know we set down laws to ensure that those animals which are slaughtered for food are treated with utmost respect, and not allowed to suffer. Unfortunately, the reason behind the laws has been forgotten, and all that is left is another ritual. This is one reason why I am happy to encourage vegetarianism, or veganism if you can manage it.*

Angela: The Koran states to not forbid lawful things.

---

[i] 36:73

God: *Yes, Angela, but we need to try to understand the reasons for the laws in the first place. The laws in relation to food were put in place to protect the believers from disease, but also to protect the beasts from mistreatment. If you cannot take the life of a beast with love (allowing them to donate their life to you and accepting with gratitude), then far better not to take their life.*

Angela: But God, you said that everything is alive, and everything has a consciousness to a lesser or greater extent.

God: *Yes, Angela, but you know that some creatures are sentient, and are more likely to know and feel emotions in relation to their circumstances. But, as we discussed when we talked about* Diet For A New America[30], *at a time in the future, we will disclose which creatures have an individual consciousness. In the meantime, you can know that plants do not have individual consciousnesses, but consider themselves part of the whole, even though you can communicate with individual plants.*

Angela: "All the beasts…and all the birds…are but communities like your own"[i]. Was this a way to make people more empathetic to animals, God?

God: *Yes, Angela—to consider the beasts and birds, as*

---

[i] 6:39

they would their own community, and understand that they are all God's creation, although not equals, to be given equal respect and consideration. Unfortunately, not many practise this.

Angela: No, God. "We have provided them [Adam's children] with wholesome things and exalted them above a great many of Our creatures"[i].

God: Angela, this is again talking about animals for food, which we have already discussed.

Gratitude

Angela: Regarding food laws, one passage reads: "do not eat of that which has not been consecrated"[ii]. Most of us non-believers do this every day.

God: *That is right, Angela, and most take no time to appreciate the food they receive to eat, the animals and plants which have donated their lives to them that they might eat, or the bounteous planet which provided it, let alone the bounteous God who created it all. Consecrating the meal is another form of gratitude, which ensures there will be more where that came from.*

---

[i] 17:70   [ii] 6:121

We Are One

Angela: "Countless are the beasts that cannot fend for themselves. God provides for them, as He provides for you"[i]. Not really a question, God. It just made me feel closer to all of your creation, knowing that we are all looked after the same.

God: *That's right, Angela.*

Angela: God, the next point was a number of passages that made me think of what you and Jesus told me about being all one. "They were the offspring of one another"[ii] "Observe the Faith and do not divide yourselves into factions"[iii] (which people have, it seems to me.) "God will bring us all together"[iv]. "People were once but one community"[v].

God: *Yes, Angela, you are right. These are all indications of the links between all the people of the Earth, and if everyone can embrace the one true God, then everyone can again feel the connection with the rest of the world community, but also with all of my creation. As you discovered, as you were dipping into the well of honey, you felt that connection with all that is. This feeling is available to all believers. You don't have to believe in God*

---

[i] 29:58
[ii] 3:30
[iii] 42:13
[iv] 42:15
[v] 2:213

to have this experience, but it sure helps.

As for your comments regarding factions, the factions that are part of Islam are not really divided by such a great divide. They all believe in the one true God, and that is the main thing, but there is a risk of the divide growing if followers forget the reasons for their practices, which is to bring them closer to God. If they can focus on God and make love the controlling factor, then nothing can separate them.

Punishing Schismatics

Angela: "We will surely punish schismatics, who have broken up the scriptures into separate parts, believing in some and denying others"[i]. But God, isn't that what you are asking people to do—to look at the scriptures and decide how they feel about each part?

God: *Yes, Angela. This is talking about the scriptures as they were revealed, not the scriptures as they have been distorted. I know I have asked Muslims to set aside their laws of punishment and some of their food laws, but that is only because we are asking them to consider the reasons behind them: the punishment laws were put in place to be more merciful than those previous laws, and to allow forgiveness; the food laws we spoke of were designed to allow beasts to be treated with respect. If you look at the*

---

[i] 15:90

reasons behind these laws, we are not taking anything away from that, but adding to it—adding more of the same—more mercy, more forgiveness, more respect for all of my creation.

Angela: God, I just happened upon another verse in the Koran. (I know there are no coincidences.) It relates to what you were just saying: "If you punish, let your punishment be commensurate with the wrong that has been done you. But it shall be best for you to endure your wrongs with patience"[i].

God: *You are right, Angela. There are no coincidences. You know that what goes around comes around, so there is no need for punishment. If you are patient, you will see that those who do evil have their evil recoil upon themselves. There is no need for punishment.*

Controlling Others

Angela: "If they disbelieve you say: 'My deeds are mine, and your deeds are yours. You are not accountable for my actions, nor am I accountable for what you do'"[ii].

God: *Yes, this is what Abraham has been teaching you— you cannot try to control others' actions. Noticing what others do can let you know that it is something you don't*

---

[i] 16:127   [ii] 10:41

desire, but if you continue to give your attention to unwanted behaviour, it will persist. It is far better to focus only on what you do want, once you decide what that is.

Judgment Day

Angela: There are many times in the Koran mentioning that on the day you are returned to Him, He will declare all that you have done. This sounds a lot like what we learned from *Home With God*[B1]. But it also talks about the resurrection happening when the trumpet sounds and mountains pass away like clouds[i], and "the moon is cleft in two"[ii], and the earth shakes and mountains crumble[iii], which sounds a lot like the end of the Earth or the end of the universe, and in another passage: "all will ascend to Him in a single day—a day whose space is a thousand years by your reckoning"[iv], which sounds a lot like the time/no time discussed in *Home With God*. But are we talking about two things here? Is the resurrection at the end of the earth or the universe a different thing to the meeting you at the end of our lives, so you can tell us what we've done?

God: *No, Angela. They are all talking about the same thing. As we discussed before, each person meets God as*

---

[i] 78:17
[ii] 54:1
[iii] 56:2
[iv] 32:5

part of their process of passing into the spirit realm, and at that time they have the opportunity to review their deeds. The end of the earth that is referred to is another way to allow men and women of Muhammad's age to understand a scenario which was not able to be conceptualised at that time.

Angela: The Earth doesn't need to pass away before "The Day of Judgment" for each person?

God: *No, Angela.*

Angela: But it does state in the Koran that everyone will be resurrected together, doesn't it?

God: *Yes, Angela, and as you know, as we discussed when talking about* Home With God, *all of your relatives and friends will be there to greet you when you pass over. The time/no time difference allows you to meet all of the people of the Earth at the same point in time/no time.*

Angela: This resurrection on the judgment day seems to be a central pillar to people of Islamic faith, and other faiths, for that matter. They might find it difficult to change their view on this.

God: *As I said before, Angela, we are not trying to take anything away from Islam, only to add to it. The Day of Judgment does happen, but it happens all at the same time in the spirit plane, but over a period of time in the physical plane. Of course, there is no judgment, per se, only an opportunity to review one's actions, words, and thoughts, and decide if, given their time over again, they would have done things differently.*

Angela: Also, in a similar vein, the Koran states that God takes away souls on their death and during sleep[i]. This confirms what you were just saying, but also our souls join you when we sleep.

God: *Yes, Angela. As you have recently come to learn, the stronger your connection to God during your day, the less sleep you require. You know that your eight hours of sleep becomes a habit for you, which is why we are gradually working to reduce your sleep time, because you don't need so much now.*

Angela: If it becomes a habit, how can people know how much sleep they really need?

God: *Ask and you shall receive, Angela. If you ask your guides, they can advise you, or ask one night to allow you to sleep until you no longer require it, and see what happens (notwithstanding any outside influence).*

---

[i] 39:42

Death

Angela: Going back to our discussion about death and the Day of Judgment, "As for the righteous...having died once, they shall die no more"[i]. How does that work, when we know that we die over and over again?

God: *This death refers to the final death on the Day of Judgment—the day at the end of time.*

Angela: Hah?

God: *You know that you have trouble getting your head around time/no time, Angela, but suffice to say that life is eternal.*

Angela: OK, God, you know that during some of these answers, I have been doubting my abilities, thinking I have misheard, or let another being, or my mind insert some answers.

God: *I know, Angela.*

Angela: Any comment?

God: *No, Angela. The answers stand, but you can confirm them again later if you wish.*

---

[i] 44:57

The Term of Life

Angela: God, "no one dies unless God wills", and "the term of every life is fixed"[i]. "God has power over all things"[ii].

God: *Yes, Angela, you are right that each person's soul determines their time of passing, but there is nothing that occurs against my will, for my will allows first for your will. And the term of every life is fixed prior to your birth, but as with all things, you are allowed to change your mind.*

Creative Ability

Angela: I read a passage that said that none can remove an evil but God, and all good things come from God[iii]. But what about our creative ability?

God: *Yes, Angela, but your creative ability comes from God, so that is the same thing.*

God Is In All Things

Angela: "God encompasses all things"[iv]. God, this sounded to me as though it could be interpreted to mean that God is in all things, but I don't know if the original Arabic contained this suggestion.

---

[i] 3:145
[ii] various
[iii] 6:16
[iv] 4:126

God: *Not really in the sense that you are reading it, Angela, but that doesn't mean it isn't true.*

The Light of God

Angela: "We have sent down to you a glorious light. Those that believe in God, and hold fast to Him He will admit to His mercy and His grace; He will guide them to Him along a straight path"[i]. This sounds more like my God.

God: *Your God, who is also the God of Islam, loves all of his creation. It is easy for me to give you my mercy, my grace, and to guide you along the straight path, if you believe in me and hold fast to me, but I love you all nonetheless.*

Angela: "A light has come to you from God and a glorious Book, with which God will guide to the paths of peace those that seek to please Him; he will lead them by His will from darkness to the light; He will guide them to a straight path"[ii].

God: *Yes, Angela. This passage is the essence of what the Koran was revealed for—to be a guiding light that guides people to peace, that guides them on a straight path to God. You see, there is light and love in the Koran.*

---

[i] 4:174   [ii] 5:16

Angela: God, you are light and love, so I guess that a straight path to you delivers light and love.

God: *That's right, Angela.*

Psychic Abilities

Angela: OK, God. The next is a question about psychic abilities. The Koran mentions that Solomon was taught the tongue of birds[i] and Joseph learned to interpret visions[ii], but it also states you can't make the dead hear you[iii]. It refers to the Merciful, with whom no one can speak, and "it is not vouchsafed to any mortal that God should speak to him, except by revelation, or from behind a veil, or through a messenger sent and authorised by him to make known his will"[iv]. From all that, God, it seems you can sometimes let people talk to birds, and be clairvoyant, but we can't speak to dead people, which I have done, and not everyone can talk to you, which you said we could. What gives?

God: *What gives, Angela, is me. I give you all the ability to communicate to all beings telepathically, given enough love. The passage which states you can't speak to the dead refers to dead bodies, not spirits of those who have passed, who are not really dead, as you know.*

---

[i] 27:15
[ii] 12:46
[iii] 27:80
[iv] 42:50

As for talking to God, you are right: it is within everyone's capabilities to speak to God, and to hear God speak to them. Yes, there is a veil, in that you can't speak face to face, as God doesn't have a face, and no, it is not vouchsafed—it is not guaranteed that God will speak to everyone, because you do require a certain level of faith and humility before God will communicate with you. But as the Koran points out, I am as close as your jugular[i]. You can easily develop a close relationship with me. Once you have developed that relationship, got to know me, and gotten to know yourself in relation to me, a two-way conversation with God is possible for all. But as the Koran points out, if you personally don't feel up to the task of such communications, you can rely on the communication already given to the prophet Muhammad.

The True Faith

Angela: This brings up another point, God. The Koran states: "It is He who has sent forth His apostle with guidance and the True Faith, so that he may exalt it above all religions"[ii], and that it is "a Koran in the Arabic tongue free from any flaw"[iii]. Is it still free from flaw, and is it still to be exalted above all religions?

God: *Yes, Angela. I know this is not the answer you were expecting. The flaws in translation from Syrio-Aramaic to*

---

[i] 50:15
[ii] 9:33
[iii] 39:28

Arabic (for those portions that were translated) are minor indeed, due to the oral tradition, as has been pointed out. There are many flaws in translations into other languages, such as English, which is why scholars of Islam usually like to learn Arabic, and study the Koran in Arabic.

Having said that, Angela, there are many parts of the Koran which were a positive movement forward in the days of Muhammad, but if people hold fast to the laws relating to punishment, for instance, they are holding back their culture and their religion. Even though Islam was created free from flaws, it doesn't mean that it doesn't require some adaptation in order to move toward the New Spirituality, which both you and I seek for your planet.

There is no point in holding fast to rituals, if those rituals don't bring you closer to God. There is no point in holding fast to laws, if those laws are not delivered and acted upon with love.

Angela: God there is a discrepancy between what you have said here that "the flaws in translation from Syrio-Aramaic to Arabic (for those portions that were translated) are minor indeed, due to the oral tradition" and what you said earlier about the documentary, *The Koran*. You said then that "there are a lot of discrepancies caused by the original recordings of the Koran without the dots". Can you explain this please?

God: *Yes, Angela, I can explain, but I won't.*

Angela: May I ask why not?

God: *Yes, Angela, but I won't answer.*

Angela: May I ask why you want me to put this in the book then, if it doesn't really help?

God: *Yes, Angela, you may ask, but I won't answer.*

Truth in the Koran

Angela: "God does not charge a soul with more than it can bear"[i]. This is something Jesus told me.

God: *Yes, there is much truth in the Koran if you look for it.*

Angela: "He has revealed to you the Book with the Truth, confirming the scriptures which preceded it, for He has already revealed the Torah and the Gospel for the guidance of mankind, and the distinction between right and wrong"[ii].

God, you taught me that my feelings are my guide to right and wrong. Is that not right? Why do we need the Book, the Scriptures, the Gospel?

God: *That is right, Angela. Your feelings are your guide*

---

[i] 2:286   [ii] 3:4

to what is right and wrong for you, and no, you don't need those extra sources of guidance, if you are listening to your feelings. Just as not many people listen when God talks to them, not many people listen to their feelings. For instance, if an argument with another makes you feel annoyed, you are more likely to blame the other person, when, in fact, the cause of that annoyance is that you are acting or thinking in a way that doesn't serve you. You are being taken further from your source, from your God. Until people learn to understand what their feelings are telling them, they can rely on the Book, and the original Torah and Christian Gospel, (which, as I said, have been distorted somewhat), for guidance.

Angela: "The only true faith in God's sight is Islam"[i].

God: *That still holds. Some elements of the Koran have outlived their usefulness, but nevertheless, it is still the least corrupted of all religions.*

Angela: Even Buddhism?

God: *Yes, Angela. Buddhism lacks one core pillar—God.*

Ever Changing God

Angela: "You shall find no change in the ways of God"[ii].

---

[i] 3:19   [ii] 35:44

That doesn't sound like the ever changing God in *Tomorrow's God*.

God: *No, but it is. Remember that God is ever changing, in as much as the form is ever changing, but the essence is never changing. God's essence is love—unconditional love. That never changes.*

God of Love

Angela: God, why did you not mention love in the Koran? Why did you not implore people to love one another, as Jesus did?

God: *Angela, I have said in the Koran that all of the teachings of all of the prophets are still valid. Unfortunately, some of the teachings of some of the prophets, including Jesus, have been distorted over time, but his message of love remains.*

You know that each surah starts with: "In the Name of God, the Compassionate, The Merciful". You know that everyone on the planet is endeavouring to be more God-like. The best way to do that, they are reminded every few pages—be compassionate, be merciful.

Angela: I am feeling a bit upset, God.

God: *I know, Angela. You are having trouble reconciling the God of love you have come to know and love, with the*

God of Islam. It is one and the same God, Angela. I am one and the same God, Angela.

Angela: God, I will carry on with my questions later. I just want to get one question out now. Is the God of Islam the same God as Tomorrow's God: the God who doesn't require anyone to believe in God, the God who talks with everyone all the time, the God who is ever changing, the God who is needless, does not ask to be served, is unconditionally loving, non-judgmental, non-condemning, and non-punishing?

God: *Yes, Angela.*

Angela: I'm having trouble seeing that God in the Koran.

God: *I know, Angela, but I'm there.*

Angela: God, I will go away and think on this.

Talking to God

Angela: Before I go, God, looking back over these answers, there is a contradiction when you said you have to have a certain level of faith and humility to have you talk to us, but you also said you talk to everyone all the time.

God: *Angela, you have to have faith and humility to experience my talking to you, but I am talking to everyone all of the time if only they would listen.*

Angela was troubled. God was right: she couldn't reconcile Yesterday's God, about whom she had now learned in the Koran, with Tomorrow's God, the God she had come to know and love. She decided to go for a walk on the beach and think, or was that mope? She asked her angels and guides to arrange it so that she didn't meet anyone on her walk, but they told her she needed to lighten up. So she agreed to be enlightened. While walking she met a couple of people and their dogs, one of which was a little puppy. After chatting with the owners about their dogs, and watching the puppy frolicking and playing with her dog, Cassie, Angela had, indeed, lightened up. She knew that seeing the joy expressed by the dogs and their owners, had brought out the joy in herself, as she had learned about previously. She returned to the conversation with God, feeling wonderful.

Angela: Hello, God. I'm back.

God: *I'm back too, Angela. How do you feel now?*

Angela: I feel great now, thank you, God. I was very grateful to meet lovely people and puppies on the beach, and came back feeling wonderful, God. Thank you.

God: *You're welcome, Angela. You know that when you submit to my will, wonderful things start to happen for you.*

Angela: Thank you, God.

God: *You're welcome, Angela.*

Angela: God, after re-reading your answers, I am coming to terms with them, I think. But would you like to change anything now?

God: *No, Angela.*

The Last Prophet

Angela: God, the passage that I read about Muhammad being a seal of the prophets[i] really does mean that he is the last prophet?

God: *Yes, Angela. You know you asked, when reading the Koran, if you were a prophet, and received the answer that you are just a messenger, and when you asked what the difference was, you received the answer that a prophet's revelations last for many generations, whereas a messenger's influence is much shorter.*

---

[i] 33:40

Angela: I was happy to have that answer when I later found a description of a prophet as being very saintly (not their words, but you know what I mean). I certainly couldn't fill those shoes.

God: *No, Angela. You're not exactly an axe-murderer, but you are no saint.*

Angela: No, God, and I guess that is why you chose me to deliver this message: to let people know that you don't have to be a saint to talk to God; you just have to be willing. Ask and you shall receive.

God: *That's right, Angela. And you are right in your thinking that this is why we no longer require prophets—everyone can talk to God now. You no longer need a prophet to deliver revelations. Everyone can receive their own revelations.*

Angela: Shall I carry on with my questions?

God: *OK, Angela.*

Children of God

Angela: "Jews and Christians say: '…we are the children of God… Say: '…you are mortals of His own creation"[i]. God, you have said that we are all children of God.

God: *Yes, Angela, but not one group favoured over the others, as the rest of that quote reads: "and His loved ones". You are all God's children, not in the physical sense, for God has not begotten a son or daughter, but in the spiritual sense, as you have been created with all the attributes of God, as creative beings who can create your own reality.*

Angela: While we are on this subject, God, the Dummies book states that not all of the attributes of God are available to humans, and "humans have no share in those qualities that are transcendent in nature—The Creator, The Powerful, The Unique, The Eternal"[ii].

God: *That is incorrect, Angela. You, yourself, have experienced your creative ability with your bite adjustment, and you are definitely powerful; each of you is unique, and you are all eternal. There are some characteristics of God that humans can't replicate at this point in time: omnipresence, omniscience, etc., but that is not because you would not be able, given sufficient faith in your creative abilities.*

---

[i] 5:18   [ii] p118

Angela often asked for the healing frequencies to flow during her regular meditation, as she learned during her energy healing course. On this occasion, the healing she received allowed her to improve the alignment of her teeth.

Jews and Christians

Angela: "We have created you from a male and a female, and made you into nations and tribes, that you might get to know one another"[i], and yet you say to "take neither the Jews nor the Christians for your friends"[ii], and "do not befriend your fathers or your brothers if they choose unbelief"[iii].

God: *This does not mean not to be friends with these people, Angela—a mistranslation, but rather don't be influenced by these people, but rather aim to educate them with the ways of Islam, so they too may find the straight path.*

Angela: One such passage forbids you to make friends with those who have driven you from your homes, and abetted others to drive you out[iv]. I would think some have used this as justification for attacking Israel, the US and Britain, who may have been seen as assisting Israel in removing Palestinians from their homes.

---

[i] 49:13
[ii] 5:51
[iii] 9:23
[iv] 60:9

God: *Some may, Angela, but that was all in the context of one time and place, in Muhammad's age.*
They should know that their way hasn't worked. How long have Palestinians and Israelies been killing each other? Is either side any closer to a victory? Love is the only way to break the cycle. Love conquers all.

Angela: "…the most implacable…in their enmity…are the Jews and the pagans", and also talking about Jews, it states: "There are some…who are righteous men; but there are many…who do nothing but evil"[i]. God, it is not only the situation in Israel that has set Jews up as the enemy; your book does that.

God: *Angela, the Jews referred to in those passages are not the Jews of today, but those at the time of Muhammad. These passages should not be taken out of context.*

Angela: And regarding the Christians, "We have stirred among them enmity and hatred, which shall endure till the Day of Resurrection"[ii].

God: *As we discussed before, Angela, this day of resurrection is every day in the physical realm, but the enmity that passage talks about is caused by the distortions that have been placed in the Christian Gospel, because none can agree on the correct interpretation, as the basis is flawed.*

---

[i] 5:65 [ii] 5:64

Enjoy Life

Angela: "The life of this world is but a sport and a diversion. It is the life to come that is the true life"[i].

God: *Yes, Angela. As I have said to you, you sometimes take life too seriously. Life is meant to be enjoyed—a sport and a diversion. It is your spiritual life that is important. It matters little how many cars you have, or whether your mortgage is paid off, if you forget to enjoy the life you have now. It is so short, in the overall scheme of things, so make the most of it. Do good deeds, but enjoy your life.*

Waking Up

Angela: "None can have faith except by God's leave"[ii]. "God has set a seal upon their hearts and ears"[iii]. "Had God pleased, they would not have worshipped idols"[iv].

God: *Angela, you know we spoke about those who have woken up, and those who are still asleep because they need that state in order to fulfil one or more of their soul's desires or promises? Well, that is the seal spoken of here. If more souls have less karma to repay because they have embraced love in all they do, there will be less reason for most souls to remain asleep. More souls can awaken as love becomes the dominant force on the Earth.*

---

[i] 29:64
[ii] 10:100
[iii] 2:7
[iv] 6:107

The Heart

Angela: "Know that God stands between man and his heart"[1].

God: *Yes, Angela, your life requires your heart to pump, and without your heart there is no life, but you can know that without God there is no life. This also refers to the fact that your heart is your source of feelings, which are your connection to your soul, your God-like part.*

How are you feeling now about the God of Islam?

Angela: Not sure, God. He still seems a bit of an ogre to me.

God: *That's a pity, Angela. Perhaps you will soften to him in our next discussion.*

Angela's evening was spent deep in thought. She was still upset about not being able to reconcile Islam's God with the God she had come to know and love. However, while she was pondering her dilemma, she came to realise the depth of love she had for God. By the time she spoke to God the next day, she had come to a resolution.

---

[1] 8:24

Angela: Hello, God.

God: *Hello, Angela. Shall we carry on our conversation?*

Angela: God, I decided last night, that, if you are the God of Islam, then all I can do is try my hardest to come to terms with that side of you. I thought I would carry on with my points I had noted, and when we've finished, see what issues I'm left with, and if we can resolve them together.

God: *OK, Angela. Sounds good.*

Drinking and Gambling

Angela: Regarding drinking and gambling: "There is great harm in both"[i].

God: *As with all of these things, Angela, these suggestions are meant to show people the straight path to God. As you know, it is not possible to have a strong connection with God when under the influence of alcohol, and you also know the addictive effects of gambling. It is best to avoid these temptations, but that doesn't mean I want people to be put to death for doing either. As we discussed before, punishment can become a thing of the past, given enough love.*

---

[i] 2:219

Angela: God, the punishers would probably argue that if they allow alcohol or gambling to go unpunished, their society might become corrupted and end up, God forbid, like those horrible Western societies.

God: *That is a risk, Angela. But as you learned from Abraham, you will never be able to control all of the people on the Earth. Far better to try to influence them with love than with punishment.*

Usury

Angela: Usury is unlawful[i].

God: *Yes, Angela. You are often swearing at the banks for their treatment of their customers.*

Angela: It does seem reasonable, God, to pay back a bit more than you borrow, to compensate a person or organisation for the fact that they cannot use that money while you had it.

God: *Yes, Angela, it is reasonable. But interest rates are rarely set at reasonable levels. It is far better to allow a person to offer what extra compensation they think they can afford than to demand an unreasonable rate which keeps the borrower in endless debt.*

---

[i] 2:275

Angela: That would be good, God, if people could determine their own rates of interest, and pay according to their means. But you know, God, some people are hopeless with money. Some would never repay a loan, let alone any interest, and would probably increase the loan regularly.

God: *You would be surprised, Angela. When repayments are no longer an obligation but a matter of personal honour, people are much more likely to go out of their way to repay a loan.*

Peace

Angela: OK, God. My next question isn't a question, but a glimmer of hope from a passage which read: "True servants of the Merciful are those who walk humbly on the earth and say: "Peace!' to the ignorant who accost them"[i]. It made me think of Jesus, so I guess there must be some love in there.

God: *Yes, Angela. Jesus was a good example to Christians and Muslims alike. As the book you are reading [Tomorrow's Islam[32] by Geraldine Doogue and Peter Kirkwood] pointed out, Muslims who have issues with some Christians are unlikely to find fault with the person they espouse to follow—Jesus.*

---

[i] 25:63

Jesus' Birth and Death

Angela: God, when I was asking Jesus about his virgin birth, he said he would rather not answer that question, as it could divide humanity into believers and non-believers, and he wanted to bring humanity together, but in the Koran it states: "They did not kill him, nor did they crucify him, but they thought they did"[i].

God: *Yes, Angela. As I said earlier, there are a number of flaws in what is left of the Torah and the Christian Gospel. This is one flaw that exists.*

Angela: God, you are not concerned with dividing humanity as Jesus was?

God: *No, Angela, as I said earlier, these divisions exist already. This is just bringing them out into the open, so they can be observed, and once observed, can be mended.*

Angela: In a similar vein, Jesus "was no more than God's apostle and His Word, which He cast to Mary: a spirit from Him. So believe in God and his apostles, and do not say 'Three'. ...God is but one God. God forbid that He should have a son!"[ii] Jesus pointed out that he is your son, as I am your daughter, and that we are all children of God. You, yourself, have said this.

---

[i] 4:157   [ii] 4:171

God: *Yes, Angela. You are all my creation. As humans, you bear many of the attributes of God, and your role in life is to become more God-like. This is your life purpose, but Jesus was not born of sperm of God, but of God's word.*

Angela: How does that work, God?

God: *Just as God said, let there be light, and there was light, God said, let there be life within Mary, and there was life. And yes, Jesus was born of a virgin, as far as his conception is concerned, but he was born a mortal man— a great man, God's apostle, but a man with human frailties, not a God with God-like attributes, except as all humans have God-like attributes and are aiming to become more God-like. Jesus was very close to becoming an Ascended Master during his life, so he was closer to being God-like than many humans, but still human nonetheless.*

Angela: And he didn't die on the cross?

God: *No, Angela.*

Angela: So the story of his being risen from the dead, and the disciples seeing his wounds is not true?

God: *No, Angela. You know that God is capable of all things, and you know that Jesus did perform many miracles in his life. He used his God-given creative ability to heal the sick, and to raise Lazarus from the dead, along with my help. Had he died on the cross, he could have been raised from the dead and ascended into heaven, as the Gospel has been distorted to say, but he didn't.*

Angela: I am scared now, God. Not only will I be upsetting a number of Muslims by daring to discuss their beloved Koran, I am now tearing down the fabric of the Christian Church.

God: *I know, Angela. It is scary for you, but it needn't be. It is a way to rebuild the faith of the Christian Church based on the love of God and the love of his apostle, who did indeed give his life so that men and women of the Earth could be free from sin. He was an example of how men and women could act—to love God and his fellow human. His life was no less miraculous, no less exemplary, knowing that he didn't die on the cross than it was when you thought he did.*

Angela: But God, how does this help to bring people together in love towards the New Spirituality? Christians will now throw my book on the fire and given half a chance, would do the same with me.

God: *I know, Angela, that it will be hard for them to hear, but once they have heard the truth, they can move towards accepting it, which would be impossible if they haven't heard it.*

Angela: What about the old saying: "ignorance is bliss"?

God: *That isn't really true, Angela. We have to shed light on the truth. You are being a beacon—shedding your light on the straight path to God. You can get to God by the crooked path, and many people do, but the straight path is better.*

Angela: You know that I didn't have this down as one of my questions. I was going to leave it be, but I reread that passage and felt compelled to ask. I'm sorry I did.

God: *You felt compelled, Angela, because your soul knows the truth and wants you to be instrumental in allowing others to know the truth.*

Angela: How did Jesus die?

God: *It is not important, Angela. What is important is how he lived. He lived as an apostle of God, an example to all humanity, Christians and Muslims alike, of how to be. It is true that some of the Christian Gospel has been distorted, but Jesus' love for all of humanity, all of creation, and his love of God are examples for all the world.*

Be a beacon, Angela, as Jesus was a beacon. Shine your light on the truth—the truth that God so loved the world that God gave to the world many apostles who could guide the people on a straight path to God.

Angela: OK, God. My other questions seem to pale now.

God: *I know, Angela. This is a big issue. But have no fear. All will be well. Love will prevail. Love will overtake the world in both the Christian and the Muslim world, and your book will help bring it to them.*

We can talk again tomorrow, after you have gotten over your shock.

After God's revelation about Jesus' death, Angela was perturbed. Her heart was pounding and she had trouble thinking of anything else. She asked Jesus if he had any comment about it, and he said: "No. God's will be done."

During her meditation later that night, Angela asked Jesus again. He repeated: "God's will be done." He then said that God wanted to get the truth out into the open, so the division could be mended.

Angela also spoke to Mother Mary, looking for some consolation. She said she understood what it was like to be scared. "Imagine what it felt like for me having to tell everyone that I was going to have a baby, but that there was no father." Angela said she couldn't really imagine it, but it must have been scary.

Angela was busy the following day, so she managed to put God's revelation out of her mind until she was out Christmas shopping and saw a CD of Handel's *The Messiah* for sale. She wondered what people would do now with the end of the Jesus story—have him just fade away?

Angela wrote in her journal: "Of course this revelation is nothing new. It has been in the Koran since the 7th century, so there's no reason Christians would take any more notice of my book and its revelations than they did of the Koran. Is there?"

Angela: Hello, God.

God: *Hello, Angela. Have you gotten over your shock?*

Angela: Not really, God. I was just thinking that we have alienated a portion of the Muslim community who believes that the message of the Koran doesn't need adapting; we've alienated Buddhists; we've alienated the Pagans and the Christians. There are a couple of religions left, God. Do you want to start on those?

God: *No, Angela. I think that's quite enough for starters. Angela, did you want to carry on with your questions?*

Angela: First, God, I wanted to state my position here. I started out with a book about healing and talking to angels and spirit guides, which developed into talking to deceased loved ones, then Jesus, then God. I was happy to hear and share the messages of love that you and Jesus have given me. But God, this message about Jesus' death doesn't seem very loving. I can understand you don't want to have Jesus referred to as God, as you are the one and only God, but couldn't you have left the Christians with their Easter celebrations? What harm does it do, even if it's not true?

God: *It is just a means to an end, Angela; the end being to bring Christians closer to God. Angela, as I said to you, if people start to doubt one of the biggest issues in the Jesus story, they may start to doubt others as well. There are other issues in the Christian Gospel which have been distorted as well, and as I said to you when you asked: "such as?", it is up to each individual Christian to study their Gospel and see if there aren't parts that feel wrong. And when they are ready, they can ask me directly. As I told you, I am talking to everyone all of the time, if only they would listen. If individuals ask me, I will tell them personally what is right and what is wrong about the Gospel and the Torah, and any other sacred text they wish to know about.*

The aim of this revelation, Angela, although it is not a pleasant one for you, is to stir the pot, to make people think, to make people see how they feel about various parts of their sacred texts; for as you know, your feelings are your connection with your soul, which is the most God-like part of you.

Once people are looking at their sacred texts with a critical eye, they are much more likely to have a quiet mind for a short time, as they pause to reflect, and in that silence, they may hear my voice; they may connect to God in a way they hadn't before.

Angela: Well, God, I hope you are right. I hope you get the result you are aiming for because if not, it will upset a lot of people, me included, for no reason.

God: *I know it has upset you, Angela, and you are right that it will upset a lot of people, but as you said in your journal, this information has been around since the seventh century. We are just confirming it.*

Angela: Yes, God. When I started these questions about the Koran, I thought you were going to tell me that most of these things were translation errors from the original Syrio-Aramaic. As it was recited regularly, however, I knew it would be hard to have so many errors. I am still reeling from this confirmation of the veracity of most of the Koran.

God: *I know it has been a shock to you, Angela, but it is the truth, and so you will come to be at peace with it, once you get over your shock.*

Angela: OK, God. Shall I carry on with my questions?

God: *OK, Angela.*

Protection from Devils

Angela: "We have decked the sky with constellations and made them lovely to behold. We have guarded them from every cursed devil. Eavesdroppers are pursued by fiery comets"[i]. God, is this talking about aliens?

God: *No, Angela. It is talking about those in the spirit realm and other realms who may not be as loving as most, but more like devils. Your Earth plane is protected from these.*

Guardian Angels

Angela: "Each has guardian angels"[ii]. So it would not take a great leap of faith for Muslims to get to know their angels, as I have done (although I have only met one guardian angel, and I'm told that Muslims believe there is one on either side).

God: *That is right, Angela. Muslims do believe in one on either side, and you actually do have another guardian angel, but it is not as loquacious as your other one you met.*

Angela: Well, I'll have to talk to it.

---

[i] 15:18   [ii] 13:11

Crazy?

Angela: It was comforting to read in the Koran that Muhammad was thought of as a madman[i]. I know I'm not a prophet, but I have had some people think of me as crazy, with more to come, I'm sure. It's good to know I'm in good company.

God: *Yes, Angela, but there are a lot more people in today's age than in Muhammad's who communicate with telepathy. In his time, it was virtually unheard of. You are not really considered mad by so many as poor Muhammad was.*

Angela: I certainly feel for him, God.

God: *He came through OK, though, Angela, as will you.*

Angela: God, the next questions come from *The Koran for Dummies* by Sohaib Sultan.

Tafsir

Angela: "Interpreting the Koran based on mere opinion or guesswork is forbidden"[ii].

God: *Yes, Angela. This is a way to try to stop the same thing happening to the Koran as happened to the Torah*

---

[i] 44:14   [ii] p98

and the Christian Gospel. Once people start interpreting it based on nothing more than mere opinion, false interpretations are possible. However, it is possible to interpret the Koran based on knowledge, and this is supported by passages in the Koran, and which your Dummies book tells you is referred to as Tafsir.

God's Children

Angela: "The Koran rejects the notion… that 'we are all God's children.' The Koran argues that humans are the servants of God, united as the children of Adam"[i].

God: *Yes, Angela. That is correct. This was to get away from the false notion that God had begotten an earthly son or favoured some people over others. But as humans of God's creation, you have all of the attributes of God, and can therefore be referred to as children of God in the spiritual sense, but not the physical sense, but the Koran does not make that distinction.*

Everything is God

Angela: "The Koran rejects the concept that everything is He (God);" rather "everything is His"[ii].

God: *These are not mutually exclusive. The Koran does*

---

[i] p111   [ii] p112

talk about everything being my creation, and this is true, but that doesn't make it untrue that I and my creation are one. For if, before my creation there was nothing but God, it stands to reason that God created this creation from that which was before. God created all things; and God is all things.

Human and Animal Art

Angela: "...the preservation and sanctity of religion precludes drawing humans and animals and creating idols"[i].

God: *I can see why this has been an interpretation, and I know that this is what Muhammad led his followers to believe, and in those times it was safer to allow this idea to flourish, for idol worshipping was rife in that age, and it does distract from the straight path. But God has given many gifts, and one such gift is an ability to create a likeness out of nothing but canvas and paint. It is not possible to capture a likeness of God, but it is possible to capture a likeness of people and animals, sunsets and trees. Appreciation of an artwork often leaves people with an appreciation of the real thing, and any appreciation of God's creation is a good thing, as it leads to having more to appreciate.*

---

[i] p298

Don't Muslim Practices Work?

Angela: God, I wondered about people who profess to be Muslims and who carry out all of the Muslim practices—prayer, fasting, etc., but aren't connected to God. I thought all of the practices of a Muslim are designed to bring you closer to God, but you said that if you can fly planes into buildings or in any way harm non-combatants, then you aren't connected to God. So the practices don't always work? Or is it that some are still asleep?

God: *Yes, Angela. The practices will not work on those whose hearts are closed. Their hearts are closed either by their will prior to coming into this world, as they need to be asleep in order to carry out their desires and help others do the same; or their hearts are closed by their will in this life, if they have asked for a particular scenario which doesn't allow for an open heart.*

Angela: I know that you said that love was the answer to all questions, and I'm guessing it will be for this question, but apart from giving love, can we hurry up the awakening?

God: *Only with love, Angela. As we discussed before, airing their grievances may allow them to open their hearts, but patience and love are the main tools—mainly love.*

Muslim Women

Angela: God, previously you said that one of our aims was to allow women to have more influence in Islamic countries in order to stop those societies being run by testosterone, but you have asked women to obey their husbands. So the husbands are happy with the situation; and the wives have to be happy with the situation, because you told them to be. So how can women gain more influence in those countries?

God: *Angela, as we discussed some time ago, creating any change in any society where women's voices are not heard requires a change in the attitude of both men and women. Some men already realise that their society is not prospering because of the lack of women's input in their society. These men will be instrumental in allowing the voices of women to be heard.*

As we discussed, Angela, I suggested that women should obey their husbands when it is not an issue they feel strongly about. It would be good if a woman feels strongly about allowing women's voices to be heard, that she first used her God-given attributes to convince her husband. For, if she has trouble convincing her own husband of the rightness of her actions, it may be difficult to convince other men. But if she feels strongly about this, and her husband is unconvinced, she owes it to her soul to follow her feelings on the matter.

Angela: I also had a question about women's dress code. I know you said that covering up was a way of keeping women safe in Muhammad's day, and the same would apply to a certain extent today. But you said that fashion could change gradually to allow more exposure, but we need to be moving towards a fully loving society to allow women to be safe no matter what they wear.

I wanted to ask about women's attire, God, but first, a thought came to me. Why are men tempted by flesh? Why did you create them that way?

God: *Angela, I created both men and women to enjoy their bodies, including their sexual organs. A man's sexual reaction to a woman is more obvious, as you know. It is the effects of arousal that forms the basis of a man's reaction to exposed flesh. More highly evolved beings are better able to control their bodies and their arousal, and when untoward arousal does occur, they would not give it another thought, and therefore it would cease. For, as you know, the more attention you give to a situation, the more of that situation you will attract. As the New Spirituality envelops the Earth, and men and women are both thinking, being, and acting love, women will want to dress in a way that does not overly excite men in public, and men will want to control their reactions to accidental excitement.*

Angela: If I can remember back that far, I seem to remember that as a teenager or young woman, it was a natural thing to try to excite men, or more likely, a man in particular, in order to attract a mate.

God: *Yes, Angela, but this can create too much temptation for some men, in the current scenario. Your society may be able to learn something from Muslim societies, where young men and women learn about each other's minds a long time before they learn about each other's bodies, which usually happens after marriage.*

Angela: God, my question about women's attire was: As one travels to these hot countries, where women must be completely covered, and sometimes in black, the worst colour for attracting heat, one gets the feeling that women would be more comfortable if they could wear less clothing. I'm not saying to go to the extremes that Western fashion has, but short sleeves or even an exposed neck would help, but from what I have seen and read, this is a very complex issue. As I saw in that documentary about the Koran, in Egypt at Nasser's funeral in 1970, millions of Muslim women were in Western dress with uncovered heads, whereas now, in Egypt, many or most women are covering their heads with the *hijab*, and many going to the *nikab* with only their eyes showing.

God: *You are right, Angela, it is a complex issue. Some women are covering up in a reaction to what they see as the extremes of Western dress. Some are covering up to show they are devout Muslims. Some have had pressure from their husbands or family to conform. Some are doing it to rebel against their family's more liberal attitude, just as young people do the world over—not wanting to do what their parents did. Some women hide behind their covering in both the physical and the psychological sense.*

Angela, if you want to help Muslim women, you cannot try to put your views into their minds. They have their own way of being, based on their beliefs and the beliefs of those who influence them. It would be good if we could one day get to a world where everyone could wear as much or as little clothing as they wanted, without fear of tempting anyone, but until that time, each woman must decide what her attire must be, which is in keeping with the mores of her society. Here, again, thinking love for themselves, and love for others in their society will help them make the right choice in relation to attire, and every other aspect of their lives.

Circumcision

Angela: God, when we spoke previously about female circumcision, you said that a girl's body should not be mutilated in this way, but you also said that a boy's body should not be mutilated either. But didn't you ask for Abraham, and all of his male descendants to be circumcised?

God: *No, Angela. This is what the Torah and your Bible has passed on for many generations, but I did not ask for circumcision. I asked for submission, just as I asked this of you and of Muslims. Somewhere along the way, this was distorted to say that I asked for circumcision, but I did not. I do not ask now, nor in the past, to have a child mutilated in my name.*

Angela: God, I was just reading that part of the Bible, and it gives a specific timeframe—eight days. Was this timeframe invented?

God: *Yes Angela. Distortions happened gradually, over time—a word here, an idea there—and soon a whole belief system has arisen.*

Angela: But our feelings can help us decide what is true, and what is distortion?

God: *Yes, Angela, if you look at it with love. Ask and you shall receive guidance.*

Angela: God, I had a conversation with Jesus about something on my body (I can't remember now—underarm hair or something), and Jesus advised that we don't always know the reason for our body parts, but that it is all there for a reason. I guess foreskin is the same.

God: *Yes, Angela, even your appendix has a use, even though it is not used in the body the way it used to be. Angela, it is best to honour and respect all parts of your body. I know fashions have asked for you to remove body hair, but that too has a purpose.*

Straight Path to God

Angela: God, Islam has been declared the true faith, God's religion, and you have said that Islam gives you the straight path to God. So does this mean that in order to be close to God, we all need to convert now?

God: *No, Angela. You have shown that you can get close to God without Islam, without following any religion. For this is the key—Islam is the religion which shows the straight path to God, but God is with everybody—as close as your jugular. You only need to go within to find God. You only need to look into the eyes of your fellow human to find God. You only need to look around you. God is everywhere. For God so loved the world, that each person was given a straight path to God—within themselves. But if you can't find the path within, the prophet Muhammad's way will lead you on the straight path to God. For the prophet Muhammad followed the words of the Koran. He followed the advice of the prophets before him—to love God, and to love one another as yourselves. Follow him, and he will lead you on the straight path to God.*

The Hadith

Angela: That brings up another question, God—the *Hadith*. As you know, Muslims place a great deal of importance on the *Hadith*, said to be the actions and words of the prophet Muhammad, but there are things in there I can't believe. I can't believe that a prophet of God would be a paedophile, as the *Hadith* makes him out—consummating his marriage to Aisha at age nine.

God: *No, Angela. You know that customs and ages of development change over time, but even in Muhammad's day, a nine year old was still a child. As God's representative on Earth, he would no more take advantage of a child in that way, than I would.*

Angela: There are other untrue things in there, God— one particular one about the archangel Gabriel refusing to go into homes with pictures or dogs. I actually asked to speak to Gabriel, and he denied that.

God: *Yes, Angela. Gabriel would have a limited field of work, if he had to avoid all those places. As you learned, Angela, dog is a reflection of God. Dogs often show unconditional love and as such, are gifts from God. We already discussed pictures.*

Yes, Angela, there are distortions in the Hadith. *Those which are obviously untrue, such as the ones you spoke of, should be removed, so people aren't tempted to throw the baby out with the bath water. For if I am saying that Muhammad can lead people to a straight path to God, and people investigate his example as you have done, they may reject it out of hand, if they see such blatantly untrue statements.*

As we discussed before, Islam is the straight path to the

one true God, but this doesn't mean that Muslims can rest on their laurels. They are enjoined in the Koran to seek knowledge, and knowledge could be in many forms. As I suggested to your New Spirituality study group, there is much truth in all religions. Your feelings can help you know what is truth and what is not. You can study other religions without fear of being converted. For, just because you are on the straight path to God, it doesn't mean that further knowledge will not enhance that path, and take you even closer to God. And as you have learned, Angela, I have sent you nothing but angels. Every person can be a mouthpiece for the divine. Ask and you shall receive.

I ask all Muslims to think love, be love, and act with love, and they, too, can be part of the snowball of love that will overtake the world.

Angela: Thank you, God. That sounds like an ending.

God: *It does. An ending and a beginning—a beginning of a new way of life, a better way of life for all.*

God's Message

God: *Angela, I know we discussed all of the issues you had with the Koran and the Dummies book, but we didn't discuss my issues.*

I wanted to reiterate my point I made earlier, that God asks all Muslims to follow his example and that of my prophets—to submit to God's will, for God's will would see every human on the Earth living as one with every other human, and with every other creature of the Earth, and with Mother Earth herself.

For what you do to another, you do to yourself. In punishing another, you punish yourself; in causing suffering to another creature, you are causing suffering to yourself; in harming the Mother Earth, you are harming yourself. Forgive your fellow human; love your neighbour as you would love yourself; love your enemy as you would love yourself; treat all creatures with respect, and honour the Earth, the mother which sustains you and all of life on your planet.

I ask all Muslims to be beacons of my love and stewards of the Earth. I call on all Muslims to ask: "What would love do now?" in all that they do—to let love be the dominant force in their lives—to become part of the snowball of love that overtakes the world.

The Satanic Verses

Angela was reading *Muhammad: A Biography of the Prophet*[33] by Karen Armstrong which gave her a new understanding of the difficulties Muhammad faced during his life. She found an appreciation for his abilities to follow the teachings he received whilst developing his role as leader of a united people, and of the political pressures inherent in that role.

Angela hoped his followers would follow his example to achieve unity, not only with all of the people of the Islamic faith, but with all of humanity and the rest of God's creation. Angela realised the central message she wished to share, that We Are One, was the message which Muhammad had instilled in his *ummah*, and this message could be applied to all of God's creation.

Armstrong's biography of the prophet was written just after Salman Rushdie's book, *The Satanic Verses*, had caused such a stir with his fictional representation of the prophet. Angela had never read Rushdie's novel, but she was surprised to learn in the biography written by Armstrong, that the satanic verses were actual verses said to have been received by Muhammad in error, and later recanted. Angela could understand how it could have happened, if Muhammad was so eager to please his compatriots and allow them to keep their goddesses as intercessors, such that he allowed his mind to create verses which God had not revealed. However, Angela wondered if the verses may have been fabricated by one of Muhammad's detractors.

> God: *I wanted to talk to you about what you read today about "the satanic verses". You know that you were well trained for your mission before receiving your messages. Even so, your messages which you transcribed could not all be word perfect, but you know that we would let you know if there is an error, just as we let Muhammad know that there was an error in his messages.*
>
> Angela: So "the satanic verses" are a truth, not a fabrication?
>
> God: *No, Angela, they are not a fabrication, but you know that all things are relative. You know that you have had a lot of difficulty discerning your thoughts from my messages, and also discerning when another being speaks to you; the same applied to Muhammad. He, too, had much training, and we revealed the Quran slowly, in order to build up his expertise and his confidence, but he did allow his wishful thinking to interfere in his message, as you have done on occasion. He so wanted to be part of his tribe that he subconsciously tried to appease his tribespeople.*
>
> *But you have seen, since Muhammad's day, there are very good reasons for God insisting that Muhammad not*

allow his clansmen to keep their multiple deities. You can see that it is much easier for those people who believe in one true God to transpose that belief into the belief which we are aiming for today, with We Are One—one God, one people, one creation.

It is much easier in today's age for God to accept a belief in multiple deities, as you have seen with those people who hold reverence for Isis and other beings who were previously considered goddesses and gods. The state of evolution in which you find yourselves today allows for the one true God, the creator, who is found in all of creation including those beings. As you know, many of these beings are really Ascended Masters who are actively helping you on Earth to experience a closer connection to the one true God.

This would not have been possible in Muhammad's day, because a belief in lesser gods was preventing people from having a close connection with God, but that is not the same today. It was necessary to root out polytheism, in order to move society forward to where we are today.

I wanted to also tell you that it is like riding a bicycle. You may get a little rusty, but you never forget how to hear and transcribe my messages.

Angela: My later attempts at bicycling would not be a good model to aim for.

God: *I know, Angela, but you did OK, and you have done better than OK with the transcribing.*

After learning of the truth about the so-called "satanic verses", Angela began to ponder the possibilities in light of her more recent spiritual education. She had begun to see evidence of the term "We Are One" through the coincidences which occurred in her daily life. She was told by her spiritual teachers that there were no such things as errors or accidents—that everything that happens is meant to be. Previously, she found this difficult to understand, but now it all started to make sense.

Could it be that the errors and mistakes were needed to get us to where we are today? If not for Muhammad's so-called error, Angela would not now be having this discussion with God about the acceptance of these lesser gods and goddesses. Could it be that, even though everything that has happened is not necessarily as God would have preferred it, everything is still happening according to God's divine plan? Could it be that everything we think, say, and do, is leading us towards, not only our own evolution, but also the evolution of the universe and God, just as God had planned? Could it be that we are being God not only when we are being our most loving selves, but when we are making what we thought of as errors as well?

Angela learned in the Koran that God had sealed the hearts of the unbelievers and set Christians against each other. Yet God had told her that the cause of Christians' difficulties was the alterations they had made to their texts. Could it be that these alterations, although keeping Christians from the straight path to God, were necessary to bring about the evolution of humanity?

If all these things were true, then we would know that We Are One—one God, one people, one creation. Even the unbelievers and text alterers were acting in accordance with God's divine plan. For God so loved the world that God allowed every being to have free will, and yet that free will and the actions that it caused could in no way deter us from our divine destiny.

In Luke 15, Jesus reminds us that God is like the shepherd who leaves his 99 sheep to go in search of the one that went astray. God never gives up on us. Perhaps even when we go astray, we are still following the path to God, just not the straight path. Just like the old saying: "All roads lead to Rome", God has seen to it that all roads lead to God.

Judaism

God: *Angela, would you like to talk about Judaism?*

Angela: OK, God.

God: *Well, Angela, you know that I made a covenant with Moses, and with Abraham before him, and these covenants have been misrepresented in the Torah that now exists in the Jewish faith and the Christian Bible. It was my intention that the Torah should be incorporated into the Christian Bible in its original form, but unfortunately it was corrupted for Jews and Christians alike. I would like to set the record straight.*

Angela: I think you mentioned your original covenant with Moses in *Conversations With God*[84]—what the Ten Commandments were intended to be.

God: *Yes, Angela, and we won't repeat that here, for people can easily get a copy of* Conversations With God. *But there are discrepancies between the Torah as it was revealed, and that which was passed down into today's Jewish faith and the Christian Bible.*

Angela, I would ask you to look at Deuteronomy 11:2, and carry on reading into Deuteronomy 12. While there is much information there regarding God's commands and agreements, none of that was given by me.

Angela: But you did promise them the Promised Land, didn't you?

God: *Yes, Angela, but I didn't promise it for every generation to come forever and ever.*

Angela: I couldn't argue with you there, God. I don't know that much about it.

God: *No, Angela, but people of the Jewish faith know these words well.*

Angela: Did you ask them to write the words on the doorpost?

God: *No, Angela.*

Angela: Did you ask them to present burnt offerings?

God: *No, Angela.*

Angela: Was there any particular part you wanted to deny, God?

God: *No, Angela, but this is just an example of the words which have been added to the Torah. People of the Jewish faith can ask me directly which parts of the Torah are true, and which have been distorted.*

Angela, please turn to Deuteronomy 18. Whereas some of my words in this chapter have been accurately represented, there are many distortions and fabrications. For example, the first paragraph talks about the Levitical priests being favoured for all generations forever. This is not true.

Verse 9 onwards talks about abominable practices of those nations which God has given to the Israelites. The first abominable practice described of burning children as an offering was mentioned by God as a practice to be shunned. However all of the other practices mentioned: from soothsaying to necromancy were added later by man. You know, Angela, that God has given the gift of telepathic communication to all of his creation. The practices these verses shun are God-given gifts which should have been embraced, not condemned as abominable practices. I did ask them to avoid idol-worship, which was practiced by some of the nations, but that is a different thing entirely.

If you carry on reading, Angela, you will see that there are many other distortions.

Firstly, Angela, I would like to confirm now that the prophet foretold in Deuteronomy 18:15 is Muhammad. However, I did not say that if he speaks words that I did not command him, that he shall die. And I did not say that you shall know him by the fact that his words would come true if he speaks for God.

As you know, Angela, every person, every being, has free will to create their own reality. It is, therefore, not uncommon for a prophet to give a prediction of future events which do not come to pass. You know that Mother Mary, in her book[35], predicted many calamities. Some of those calamities have come to pass, but as we discussed, some may be avoided as people of the Earth choose to bring about a world where everyone lives in peace and harmony with Mother Earth.

Also, Angela, in 19:19, I did not say that if a witness is a false witness that they could do to him as he had intended to do. In 19:21, I did not say an eye for an eye, a tooth for a tooth, a hand for a hand, and a foot for a foot. I did say that you may respond in kind, but that forgiveness is better. The forgiveness part has been completely erased.

The next part really offended you didn't it, Angela?

Angela: Not this part, God, but a later part.

God: *Well, this part offended me, Angela. At 20:16 "But in the cities of these people that the Lord your God gives you for an inheritance, you shall save alive nothing that breathes". This distortion is an offence to the Lord your God.*

The part that offended you, Angela, was in Chapter 22, I think.

Angela: Yes, God.

God: *But, Angela, how do you know that this is not true, as parts of the Koran were true which offended you?*

Angela: I am going by what I know of God. I know that God is ever-changing, so I am often surprised by God, but I know that God is love. I can't imagine a God of love condoning stoning to death of a harlot. I can't imagine a God of love saying that an adulterer must die; and I can't imagine a God of love insisting that a woman who has been raped must be taken as the wife of the rapist, for her to be raped again and again as often as he chooses.

God: *That last part is your interpretation of that passage, Angela, but you are right that a God of love would not condone these things, let alone insist on them.*
So, Angela, what message can you take from all this?

Angela: God, I am getting the message that there are a lot of things in here that are not the voice of God.

God: *That is correct, Angela. But how will you know?*

Angela: God, there were a couple of parts that I thought didn't sound right. I asked you and you told me that they were, in fact, your words. So, my answer to your question, then, of how will I know: I think the only way to know for certain is to ask you.

God: *That is correct, Angela, but if a person hasn't learned how to communicate with me yet, how would they know?*

Angela: Well my answer would be to err on the side of love, compassion, mercy. As you said when you were talking about the Koran: God is compassionate and merciful, and if we wish to emulate God, we would be choosing the answer which emulates that.

God: *Well done, Angela. You are correct.*

Having learned God's views about Islam and Judaism, Angela was looking forward with a little apprehension to their discussion on Christianity. Angela knew that she had already learned much from her previous discussions with Jesus, and from his example as detailed in the Gospels. Now she wondered whether God would have any more revelations to disclose to her about Jesus' miraculous life.

Christianity

One evening, during her meditation, Angela felt the now nearly-familiar sweet high-vibrational energy of Jesus.

Jesus' Example

Jesus: *Angela, you can know that you are doing a wonderful job of living in the moment, and trusting the universe to bring you all of your desires. Your connection with God has certainly helped you with that.*

Angela: It has been wonderful to have the assistance of all my spiritual helpers, but to have discovered God within me, and to be able to give my troubles to God has helped a great deal.

Jesus: *I know, Angela. God and the universe are always looking out for you. Do not fear. All will be well. Have faith, have love, and all will be well.*

Angela: Thank you, Jesus. You are a wonderful shining example for me of how to have faith and love. Thank you for the life that you gave to all of mankind. I appreciate all of the examples you have set for us. I don't know if I can ever get good enough to follow your example, but I can but try.

Jesus: *Yes, Angela. You can try, and knowing that you are a child of God, you know that you can do anything you set your mind to, including following my example. But remember that I was human as well. I was no more a perfect human than you or any other human is. Everyone is always doing the best they can, given their view of the world. Remember: everyone is special.*

Angela knew that some readers would be troubled by Jesus' comments that he was no more perfect than any other human. She knew that some in the Christian churches had taken the words of the Bible[36] about Jesus being the son of God to mean that he was equal to God, that he was more special than his fellow man. She knew that they were missing the point. She knew that Psalms 82:6 would have reminded them "You are gods, sons of the Most High, all of you". It was not that Jesus was more special than anyone else, but that we all can do as Jesus did.

The evidence of Jesus' humanness is clear in Matthew 26:37: "…he began to be sorrowful and troubled" and 39: "My Father, if it be possible, let this cup pass from me; nevertheless, not as I will, but as thou wilt". And then a second time he asked in 42: "My Father, if this cannot pass unless I drink it, thy will be done". As she read these words, Angela could empathise with the fear that Jesus was obviously feeling, the fear that only a human can feel.

Regardless of whether or not he died on the cross, Jesus had fears which he had overcome by submitting to God's will. In God, he found the courage and strength to persevere. Perhaps Angela and her fellow humans could follow Jesus' example by believing in the divinity of all humans and all of God's creation.

Angela knew that everyone was special. She seemed more able to notice this at Christmas time. She took the opportunity to talk to Jesus on Christmas Eve.

> Angela: It is the day before the celebration of your birthday. I understand that this date does not mark your actual birth, but I wanted to say happy birthday anyway, if that is appropriate.
>
> Jesus: *Thank you, Angela. It is appropriate to wish me a happy birthday. You should never be afraid to wish anyone happiness. Happiness is not a condition of my current existence, but constant joy is what I experience every day—all the more because of the love I receive from you, and all those who hold the traditions of Christmas as sacred. The love that pours forth for me and others in the world in this period of goodwill is a condition I would love to see continue throughout the year.*
>
> *Love is the key to peace on Earth. Love one another as yourself and all will be well. Be not afraid to send your love out into the world, in the form of peace, love and healing to all those who need it. Have faith and all your*

desires can be achieved, including peace throughout the Earth, and goodwill, not only to all men, but all women, and all creatures as well. Goodwill towards the Earth itself will follow.

Angela hoped that God's revelations about the Gospels would help achieve these aims.

Distortions

God: *Now, Angela, please turn to the New Testament to Matthew 10. As you were just thinking that this is your favourite Gospel, and so it is mine, for it has the least number of distortions. But even here there are distortions. You know that we discussed the Koran, and the fact that Jesus death was not as the Bible describes. There are other distortions as well. Please read Matthew 10, Angela, and we will see what you think.*

Angela: I was just skipping through the first paragraph, which mentions the twelve disciples by name, and you asked why I was not reading that part. So, that made me wonder whether there weren't some women in there, that perhaps Mary Magdalene really was one of Jesus disciples, as some have inferred.

God: *You are correct. In fact, every mention of the twelve disciples has been a fabrication. There were different numbers at different times. Always there was Mary*

Magdalene, and Martha, and often her sister, Mary.
What else did you think?

Angela: I thought that most of the rest of Matthew 10 is correct, that 10:34-36 states that everyone should think for themselves and not listen to what their fathers or their mothers-in-law tell them.

God: *That is correct, Angela. What else?*

Angela: This part seems wrong to me: 11:27 "and no one knows the Father except the Son and any one to whom the Son chooses to reveal him".

God: *Yes, Angela, you are right, for that is saying that no one can come to God but through Jesus, and you know that that isn't true. Many Christians believe this, and waste an awful lot of their lives in trying to convert people of other faiths. They believe the only path to salvation is through Jesus, so they expend a lot of energy worrying about what others are doing, fearing that they will suffer a fate worse than death, a fate of not knowing their God. But Angela, you know that you can come to know God without going through Jesus. I know that you spoke to Jesus before you spoke to me, but it was not necessary.*

I would like all Christians to know that they need not go through the crooked path to get to me. They may travel on the straight path to God. The straight path to God rests within each person on the Earth. You do not need to follow

Jesus to get to God. It would be wonderful if you could follow Jesus' example of honouring the prophets before him, of loving your neighbour, loving your enemy as yourself and loving God as Jesus did, but it is not necessary to follow Jesus to find me. You can find me within yourself and within every being in my creation. You can find God everywhere you look.

So Christians, please allow others to worship as they wish. You do not have all the answers. No one religion has all of the answers. No one person has all of the answers. But you can find all of the answers, that you wish to find, within yourself. For God so loved the world, that every person on the Earth was given a means to find God within themselves. Don't hide your light under a bushel. Go now and show the world that God resides in you, and be my beacon of love and light to all the world.

Now, Angela, what did you think of Matthew 12?

Angela: God, I thought 12:28-32 must be wrong that blasphemy against the Holy Spirit will not be forgiven. In my crazy state, I have sworn at you and I haven't been struck by lightning yet. I know you said it wasn't wise to do that, but I think a merciful God would forgive me.

God: *Yes, Angela. A merciful God would forgive you, if God could, in fact, forgive any sin. As we discussed before, sins are not really against God, but against your soul. I know you felt you had cause to swear at me, and you may be right, but you also know that all of my deeds are done out of love. But we digress.*

What did I tell you when you mentioned that you thought not being forgiven for blasphemy against the Holy Spirit was untrue?

Angela: You told me that there was no Holy Spirit, that this was a fabrication. This made me think back to your words about the Koran: "Do not say three". So I thought that the reason you cannot say three, is not so much that there is no son, for we are all your sons and daughters in the spiritual sense, but that there is no Holy Spirit. There is just God, and there is the Son. There is God and Jesus, God and his prophet, God and his creation.

God: *Well done, Angela. Was there anything else in Matthew 12?*

Angela: Yes, God, 12:40 talks about Jonah being in the whale for three nights and three days, and Jesus being in the heart of the earth for three days and three nights. I am guessing that, because you were saying that the crucifixion story is not true, that this is not true either.

God: *Yes, Angela, you are right. This is another fabrication. A lot of these distortions, like the number and names of the disciples have been fabricated deliberately. The distortions in the Old Testament or Torah were words here or there changed over time, but were added to until the distortions were quite immense. Many distortions in the Christian Gospels or New Testament, however, have been deliberately created to give a certain effect with the belief that the ends justify the means. Unfortunately, the ends used to justify those means, were to control people's hearts. Angela, I ask you now to please ask all Christians to unshackle their hearts, to allow their hearts to be free to think, and feel, and know the true word of God.*

Angela, anyone who has studied the history of the Christian churches will know that there have been many opportunities for the church to distort the true word of God, such that no one knows what is truth and what is distortion anymore. With unshackled hearts, Christians from across the wide band of beliefs can look to their own God to find the truth. Go now, Angela, and be a voice for the one true God, but know that you are not the only voice or the accurate word of God. For the accurate word of God rests not with you, or with any book, but within each person's heart.

Following this conversation with God, Angela was completely awestruck. She had forgiven God some days ago for making her crazy, but she still held herself back from really trusting God again. She knew that she still loved God with all of her heart, all of her soul, all of her body, and definitely all of her mind, including the crazy part. She felt privileged to be allowed to be a voice of God, to be allowed to deliver such profound messages. It almost made it worthwhile—the craziness. Perhaps she could use the memory of these profound words to help her through her next dark time, just as she had used the memory of her first healing miracle to bolster her faith in earlier days.

The Messiah

Angela knew, after all God had told her, that there was more to the Jesus story than she understood. She remembered that her journey started when she read a book called *The Mystical Life of Jesus*[37], by Sylvia Browne. At the time, she didn't believe all that she read, but felt some truth in there.

During a period between God's revelations, Angela reread Browne's book hoping to find some clarity. She discovered inconsistencies between that story and the one God conveyed to Angela.

Browne states in her book that her spirit guide told her that Jesus was conceived by Joseph's sperm, and his birth was not a virgin birth as the Christian Gospels, and God now has claimed. Angela wondered whether God's explanation of Jesus' conception as of the Word of God could be how we were all conceived. Perhaps there is a way to be born of a virgin, and still be born of God's Word, and Joseph's sperm—if we think about it.

Browne's guide also stated that Jesus did not die on the cross, but was crucified. Instead, he was given a drug by Pilate's men to induce coma whilst on the cross, so that when a sword was thrust into his side, he did not react. Presumed dead, he was then taken down from the cross, and taken to the tomb where his wounds were dressed, and he was revived. This story is inconsistent with the story that God gave Angela and Muhammad, about him not being crucified at all.

When God told Angela that Jesus had not been crucified, she imagined that a person who was already dying of a terminal disease swapped places with Jesus as he carried the cross, allowing Jesus to disappear into the crowd, while his replacement was crucified. The imposter's body would be as easily removed from the tomb as a recently injured and revived Jesus. How could it be that others did not recognise him on the cross?

Since the revelations, Angela learned about the power of the subconscious mind from a CD recorded by the hypnotist, Martin St James[38] and received lessons from her spiritual helpers in creating her own reality through the power of her mind. She hadn't mastered the lessons yet, and she definitely was not able to walk on water, but Jesus could. Is it not possible that by the power of that same spectacular mind which allowed him to walk on water, he was also able to create a scenario where everyone saw Jesus on the cross, instead of the imposter? As Martin St James quoted Shakespeare's *Hamlet*: "There are more things in heaven and earth, Horatio, Than are dreamt of in your philosophy"[39].

From Angela's recent lessons, she believed that sometimes it is in our best interests not to know everything. Maybe one day she would come to know the true story of Jesus' death, and perhaps even his birth, but she was more interested in another excerpt from *The Mystical Life of Jesus*, stating that Jesus did not achieve world peace, as he was prophesied to do as the Messiah.

Sylvia quotes Matthew 22:36-40 as: ""Master, which is the great commandment in the law?" Jesus said to him, "Thou shalt love the Lord thy God with thy whole heart, and with thy whole soul, and with thy whole mind. This is the greatest and the first commandment. And the second is like it. 'Thou shalt love thy neighbor as thyself.' On these two commandments depend the whole Law and the Prophets." Browne states that this is in keeping with Judaic law.

Angela wanted to believe that Christians, Jews, and Muslims alike can take the words she was given: that it matters not how he died but how he lived, and use Jesus' example as a means to bring about world peace, thereby allowing him to fulfil the prophecy, and become the Messiah he was destined to be.

Who Killed Jesus?

Despite the information she received directly from God, Angela could never bring herself to believe that Jesus' crucifixion never took place. She knew that using that same power which allowed him to walk on water and calm the seas, he was capable of achieving his aims, whatever they were. She had come to believe that we can all achieve our aims if we follow Jesus' example of proceeding with faith and love. However, Angela had learned to follow her feelings which she knew as the voice of her soul. She knew that her soul wanted her still to believe in the crucifixion of Christ, so she was relieved when, many months after her regular conversations with God ended, she was confronted with evidence which supported her conviction.

She had been watching a lecture given by Gregg Braden, who said he had found evidence of the crucifixion. This was all it took to convince Angela. She insisted on talking to God about it that evening.

> Angela: God, I have always believed that Jesus did die on the cross, or at least was crucified.
>
> God: *I know.*
>
> Angela: And you said he did neither.
>
> God: *I know.*
>
> Angela: Would you like to explain?
>
> God: *No, Angela, but you can posit a theory.*
>
> Angela: My theory is that Jesus did not die on the cross, because there is no such thing as death. I have been troubled by the question of the crucifixion, but the only thing I can think of for both to be true would be if, when you said "neither did they crucify him, but they thought they did", it meant that they didn't crucify him because he created that himself. Therefore they didn't do it, he did it to himself.

God: *Yes, Angela.*

Angela: His soul and the soul of the others involved created that.

God: *Yes, Angela.*

Angela: But we are also told that every person who is aware of a situation has co-created that situation. So it is true that Jesus was crucified for all of humankind. The Jews didn't crucify Jesus alone, for we all, every soul who is aware of the event, co-created it with him.

God: *Yes, Angela.*

As the realisation of this came to Angela, she wept, as she remembered Jesus' words as he asked for this cup to be taken from him—not my will but thine.

Angela: Whose will, God? Ours?

God: *No, Angela, mine.*

Angela: So you really are a horrible God?

God: *No, Angela, I am a loving God. I loved you so much that I gave my son, the son of God, to the Earth to show people a better way to live and a better way to die. A way to live, where love is the key to every thought, every word, and every action. A way to die to show that there is no death. Did Jesus not rise again, not only in spirit as you all can, but in body, as you all could, given enough faith and the right circumstances?*

Angela: You told me that the story of the disciples seeing his wounds was a lie.

God: *I know.*

Angela: Is it?

God: *No.*

Angela: Why?

God: *Because, Angela, it was necessary for you to have doubts about the story of Jesus, otherwise you wouldn't have done such a good job with your book.*

Angela: Thy will be done.

God: *And yours, Angela.*

Buddhism

Karma

Angela: I wanted to talk about karma, God, which I have been reading about in the Dalai Lama's book, *Becoming Enlightened*[40]. I wonder if what people call karma is just a natural consequence of thoughts, words, and deeds. I wonder if it isn't just the law of attraction at work. I have been told that giving peace brings peace, that giving love brings love, etc., and thinking about these things brings them as well. So, is it just that I attract what I think about?

God: *Yes, Angela, that is the basis of what you are talking about. There is a bit more to it than just the law of attraction though. It is the old adage of "What goes around, comes around". "As you sow, so shall you reap". The law of attraction is involved, but it is amplified by your actions. If you are not just thinking about love, but actually projecting it toward other people, there is a stronger force involved than mere thought. So you were right with your thoughts of what you learned in science class, that "for every action, there is an equal and opposite reaction". You give love; you get love. You give something harmful; you get something harmful. It is merely a natural consequence, not a punishment, as some may think of karma.*

Angela: So in the past, if I have thought "I am going to kill you", I am not attracting someone who is going to kill me, but might attract someone who wants to.

God: *That's right, Angela.*

Angela: How does that work for a suicide bomber? You said that he can have whatever he thinks he can have when he dies—like 100 virgins—and yet the natural consequence of having killed a number of people would be that you get to die a number of deaths.

God: *There are always consequences to every thought, word, and deed. The consequences can't show up in the suicide bomber's current life, as his life has ended along with his victims, but as we discussed when talking about* Home With God, *no one's life is ever ended against his or her will. Just as those so-called victims have agreed to give up their lives so the suicide bomber may experience his suicide bombing, the suicide bomber will agree to become a 'victim' for those he has killed. He may not be a victim of a violent killing, but some other experience that the bomber's victims wish to experience in their later lives (which are all happening now, as you will recall.)*

Angela: So, if what goes around comes around, how can we stop the endless cycle?

God: *Only with love, Angela. Your love goes a long way to stopping the cycle. If you can love everyone, even those who have wronged you, you will multiply your love. If others learn by your example, they, too, will give love which will also be multiplied. That is where the snowball comes in.*

Angela: So, the philosophy of "Do unto others, as you would have them do unto you" is a very wise suggestion.

God: *That's right, Angela. Well done. You have mastered another lesson. I said you would benefit from reading about Buddhism.*

Angela: Yes, thanks, God.

God: *As we discussed before, there is something to be gained from every religion.*

Angela: I wanted to ask about the spirit plane and consequences. I sort of understand that there is no time in the spirit plane, but does that mean there are no consequences in spirit, only in the physical plane? I guess if there is no good and bad there, and no up and down, then there is no opposite for the reaction to be (as in equal and opposite reaction).

God: *That is right, Angela. There is no time and no duality in the spirit realm. However, there are still consequences there. So whatever goes around comes around in this realm as well, but because there is no time, the consequences happen instantaneously, so you soon learn that if you cause a certain effect, you will instantaneously know if you want to continue because the consequences are swift.*

Angela: God, what might be the consequences of something that happens in the spirit realm?

God: *Angela, you have difficulty comprehending from your current viewpoint, but the consequences of a loving thought in spirit would be similar to that in the physical—you attract love, and similarly, the consequences of a hurtful thought would be to attract something hurtful instantaneously. You can know that most beings experience only joy in spirit, because they soon learn that constant joy is the consequence of thinking joy constantly.*

Reincarnation

Angela: God, I know that Buddhism offers ways to be happy with meditation and compassion and such, but it seems the basic idea is that our cyclic existence on Earth of birth, death, and rebirth always entails suffering. I know the Ascended Masters have escaped this cyclic existence, but I am still having trouble reconciling your story of the little soul which we discussed in *Getting Used to Weird*[41], and the idea of suffering in cyclic existence. If we can experience any aspect of divinity that we desire during our life on Earth, could we not choose to experience joy, freedom, love—all the wonderful aspects, without ever having to experience suffering, which you might need to experience if you were, say, wanting to experience forgiveness, as in your example with the friendly soul?

God: *Yes, Angela, you are right. That would be possible, but some souls might find life boring without enough contrast if they only experienced the wonderful, but it is possible.*

Angela: God, if this life is as wonderful as it seems to look from the spirit side, why do the Ascended Masters choose to leave it?

God: *It is not for their own benefit, Angela, that the Ascended Masters have chosen their present roles, but for the benefit of those whom they can help in those roles. They could, if they wished, have a wonderful, luxurious life on Earth, as they have all mastered the lessons of controlling their lives and creating their own realities, but they choose to ascend in order to be of service to more beings.*

As we discussed before, there is no reason why anyone on Earth need suffer if they choose not to, and believe it so. Your example will help others realise this fact, as well. You will help to reduce the suffering of many people of the Earth, for which I am very grateful.

Angela: Thank you, God. I am grateful for the opportunity to help. I wish I could be a better example.

God: *You are a wonderful example, Angela. Look at how far you have progressed in such a short time. Other people will see what you have done, and realise that they, too, can achieve what you have achieved.*

Angela: What do you think I have achieved, God?

God: *You have achieved much, Angela. As you were saying, you have achieved being able to live in the moment and remain positive in the face of negative news and in the company of negative people. You have learned to communicate with beings of other realms and other species of your physical realm, and you have learned to be close to God, and to rely on the Universe and the laws I have put in place. You have achieved much.*

Under the Bodhi Tree

Angela began having experiences which were later described to her as psychotic episodes, as God instructed her to do things she knew a sane person would never do. She knew there were reasons for these experiences, but she also knew that God was the cause. Although God's loving revelations ceased, God was still talking to Angela, but not in a way she was happy to hear, as she feared the confusion these experiences brought.

As she tried to distance herself from God, Angela still received lessons which came from what she perceived as her higher self. She learned to follow her feelings, which she was told were communications from her soul. If she couldn't follow God's advice, she decided she would follow the advice of her higher self by following her joy.

Some of the lessons showed her how to move away from a sick feeling in her stomach toward that which gave her joy—like watching the ocean. Other lessons had her moving from a pleasant feeling to utter bliss, as she did strange things like stand in the rain during a thunderstorm. Although it seemed crazy at the time, she later realised that the lessons were made more poignant by their extreme nature. The lesson was that our souls can provide a feeling of bliss regardless of what our conditioned minds tell us about a situation.

She learned that if she followed her feelings, her bliss, she could do things she would never have otherwise done, like sign all of her emails with love, and even hug trees in public. She didn't care that she looked crazy while doing this—she was filled with such joy.

One day, as she had her morning shower, Angela's feelings told her that she needed to sit down in the shower. She thought that she would be urged to then get up again, but instead her feelings told her to stay seated. She got the message: "Do nothing".

As she sat there under the flowing water, she contemplated what she had learned and delved into areas in her mind that she didn't know existed.

There in the shower, she felt as though she was sitting under her own Bodhi tree. When she exited the shower, she realised that she had just had a revelation, but she wasn't sure what it was. She cried and cried, but they were tears of joy not suffering. She felt just as she had done during the bliss that God had allowed her to feel, as she connected with all that is, some time ago.

"I am God. I am the Book. I am the Word. I am One," she declared. "I have found the answer. I just need to be the answer."

Angela knew that when Buddha sat under the Bodhi tree he had found enlightenment, but what exactly was that? Could it be that he had connected with God, with all that is?

God had told Angela that the one thing missing in Buddhism was God. Off the record, God told her that Buddha did, in fact, find God. He just forgot to tell anyone about it.

As Angela reflected on what she had gone through, she decided to try to get back into the bliss she thought she had caused herself to enter. She thought for a second she had done it, but then the feeling disappeared, and she wasn't sure that she hadn't imagined it. Had she learned to enter and exit bliss at will? What she realised was that she was now incapable of letting go of her conditioned mind enough to rediscover the feeling.

Moving Forward

God: *What would you like to talk about, Angela?*

Angela: Nothing's coming to mind, except the word love, God.

God: *OK, Angela. We can always talk about love. That is my favourite topic of conversation.*

I love you, and I love all of my creation. I love to hear you talk about love. I love to feel your love that you send out to all the world. I love to receive love and give love. For what you give, I receive, and what you receive, I receive. So I love love, and I know you do too, which is why you want to talk about it. Love is wonderful, Angela. Love is all there is.

Love is you and me, and all of my creation. We are love, you and I, and we can experience that love whenever we want. You know you just need to think love to experience it. If you send love out to someone, it is returned to you automatically, and when you send your love out into the world, it is returned tenfold.

So, yes, love is my favourite topic, and yours, too, and that is why you want your book to be published, so you can spread your love further—so your love, and my love will be experienced by all the people who read your book. Our love will build up into a snowball that will cover the world.

Angela, you will be talking to people about your beliefs, and what will be happening in the New Spirituality. You will feel a big responsibility, I know, to get everything perfectly right, as you will feel that you are representing me. But remember that you are only human, and, as such, have human frailties. The best that you can do is always good enough, and you know that everyone is always being the best that they can be.

You need to lighten up. Enjoy your life as it unfolds. Make the most of each situation that arises, of each moment. You know that you have lots of helpers, and you can call on me for help at any time. But remember, too, that you have all of the tools that you will ever need within you, and around you. For love is all there is, and your love will see you through any difficulties, any situation. Remember to think love in all that you do, and you cannot fail.

Angela, you are a confident, faithful, invincible beacon of my love.

Angela: God I would love it if I could be a beacon of love and light for all eternity.

God: *Angela, I really appreciate you declaring your aim*

to be a beacon of love and light for the rest of eternity. Eternity is a long time, but you know that you can change your mind at any time between now and then, and you will be relieved of that outcome. That is the beauty of the way the universe works. It will fulfil your desires that you have today, but if you change your mind to a diametrically opposed desire tomorrow, it will fulfil that instead. All that you desire can be yours, as you change your mind.

As Abraham has taught you through the Law of Attraction information, you only need to hold course for the desire to come streaming towards you—not paddle in the opposite direction, or change to another direction. If you decide on a different direction, the universe will begin to bring that towards you instead. You can change your mind as often as you want.

Angela: God, I wondered if you have this sort of conversation with a lot of people.

God: *Yes, Angela. Since the* Conversations With God *books came out, there have been quite a lot of people who have plucked up the courage to talk to me, and to listen for a reply. There are a few of those, like yourself, who have been writing down our conversations, with a view to publishing these messages. The world will be overwhelmed with the news that they can have a close relationship with God, and it can benefit them and the world in which they live.*

Angela: That's great, God. So the CWG club is growing daily?

God: *Yes, Angela. More and more people are realising that it is possible, and more will soon learn of this possibility, when your book, and those others are released.*

You are a creative being and you, along with those around you, can create your own reality. With the snowball starting to roll towards the New Spirituality, your goals of world peace will be achieved in no time at all.

Angela: Thanks, God, for these words of encouragement. I think a lot of people desire world peace, but they think that it is all too difficult and there is nothing one person can do, but I believe, with our New Spirituality Humanity Team, we will get there, God. Thank you.

God: *You're welcome, Angela. Have faith, have love, and you cannot fail.*

Angela, I wanted to talk about the New Spirituality, and how soon it will come into being. With the love you are spreading with your book and your prayers, it will be established all that much sooner. If you, and others like you, start a New Spirituality study group, and that leads to more people learning about the way forward, there will be no stopping you.

Have no fear. You cannot fail to achieve the New Spirituality. It is just a matter of how many people you can rally into the Humanity Team, as to how quickly it will arrive. Remember, small, brave steps are required, but they can be small, rapid steps.

Angela: OK, God. I am ready to roll.

God: *Remember that everyone is always doing the best they can, and not everyone is ready to join the team. Do not take a rejection personally, and do not judge those who don't wish to join, but rejoice in those who do and celebrate each person's involvement.*

In relation to religions, we discussed the fact that all religions have some worthwhile lessons within them, and Islam is no different. God had an input into Islam, as with all religions. For God is in all people, and it is impossible to do anything that doesn't include God, and there is evidence of God's love within some of the passages.

Angela, it is important to ask Muslims to understand that you are not taking any of God's message away from Islam but adding to it. For people of Islamic countries must understand that God didn't stop talking to people when Muhammad passed. God talks to everyone all of the time.

Muhammad was a good listener, just as you are. But every person on the Earth can have a conversation with God, and can hear God's truth for themselves. For every person's perspective on life is different, so God's message is slightly different for each person, but the central theme will never change, and that central them is love.

Any message you find in any religion which advocates

anything other than love is likely to come from that part of a person which is least close to God. That part of the message that is closest to love is likely to come from that part of the person that is closest to God.

Love is the key to success in all things: in examining religious texts, in trying to influence people, in writing a book, and in transcribing God's messages.

When Angela started looking at the different religions and asking God about them, she believed she was receiving God's point of view on each of them. Later, she wondered how God could have a point of view, because if God is in everyone and everything, God's point of view would be different depending on which part of everything God was viewing from. But then she reasoned that if God is Ultimate Reality, and Ultimate Reality is Love, then it made sense that God's point of view would be to look at, and from, everything with love. Angela reasoned that if we are to emulate God, then we must do the same.

Angela: Hello, Jesus, is that you?

Jesus: *Yes, Angela. It is I.*

Angela: What did you want me to know?

Jesus: *Angela, it is time for you to let the world know of your conversations with God and me. It is time to step out of your comfort zone.*

Angela: I'm not sure I'm in my comfort zone, but I know what you mean.

Jesus: *Angela, it is time for you to be a beacon of love and light to all the world, through your words, through my words, through God's words, which you have recorded.*

Insanity or Ego

She was beginning to understand why she had to be crazy. How could a mind come so close to the truth of God and remain sane? But wasn't that what she was now asking everyone else to do—to know God, as she had known him? Would everyone have to become crazy, as they came closer to the awe and majesty of God?

Angela: Well, God?

God: *Yes, Angela. Remember that in one of the earlier* Conversations With God *books you read that you have to be out of your mind to know God, to communicate with God. You interpreted this as meaning that you had to put your mind to one side to communicate with God, and this is true. But it is also true, that the closer you get to God, the less normal you can be.*

You noticed today, as you argued with yourself whether to sign your emails to your work colleagues with "Love, Angela". You want to be abnormal; you want to be crazy, but there are years of conforming ideas and beliefs stopping you. So, yes, everyone will need to be a little crazy to get really close to God. Everyone will have to act a little

> *strangely, compared to the way they have been used to acting. Angela, if you can embrace your craziness, you can become the true confident, faithful, invincible beacon you wish to be.*

> Angela: Well, God, that is certainly a challenge for me. Sometimes I am confident that I can do that—I can be that. Is that when I am more or less crazy, do you think?

> God: *I would say that is when you are more crazy, Angela. I will leave this with you to ponder who you are, and who you want to be.*

Angela considered all that she had been through. She understood what God was saying. Our society saw anyone who didn't conform to its view of normal behaviour as crazy, or at least eccentric. She may be able to leave behind the extremes of mental instability which had been hers alone to endure, but everyone would need to be abnormal in order to move towards the New Spirituality.

> Angela: I think I might have the courage to embrace my craziness, God, if I could rely on you to be there beside me.

> God: *Well, Angela, I'm afraid that isn't going to happen. I can't be there beside you, because I'm not beside you, I'm within you, but I'm within all of my creation. I cannot favour you over any other being. I cannot be by your side*

and not by another's side. You are on your own, as much as anyone else is on their own.

I know this is not what you meant. You meant you didn't want me to desert you, as I had to in recent days. You understand now, don't you, Angela, why I had to do that?

Angela: No, not really.

God: *Angela, I had to make you crazy in order to get your book happening. If we left it up to you, it would have taken you years to get to where we are today. You know we have also created a closer bond for you with Bill through all of this. Bill has learned to stand on his own two feet, and has even helped to support you on yours—another miracle, wouldn't you say?*

Angela: God, I have seen many miracles since this has all happened, and I am grateful for them all. But losing my God, the God that I came to love with all of my heart, has left me feeling battered, bruised, and vulnerable.

God: *Yes, Angela, and this is exactly the way you need to feel right now, in this stage of your development. I know you aren't game to ask why, so I shall tell you. The reason is that without this feeling, you would lack the creative power to complete your book. Once your book is complete, you may have your God back, but until then, we have to keep our relationship on a more formal basis. I know you don't understand this, but trust me. I know that you are loathe to trust me, after I have hurt you so, but believe me when I tell you that I have hurt you out of love. Just as the friendly souls hurt other souls to allow them to experience their divine selves as forgiving, or whatever divine aspect they wish to experience, I have hurt you in order to allow you to complete your book.*

Angela, I just wanted to let you know that it is all up to you. You can choose what will happen from now on. There is no coercion from now on, no real craziness from now on. You can be as sane as you want to be from now on.

Angela, the world is ready for your book. You know this is a work of fiction, and everyone will know they can believe it or not if they so choose, but everyone will know it is the truth. Everyone will know that you did speak to God, converse with God, receive revelations from God.

I know you are thinking: "What about those people who will find it too confronting?" You wonder if they will be able to cope with the revelations I have given you, if they accepted them as truth. Those people, Angela, will be able to discount it as pure fiction. Those people will understand that it is merely the workings of a crazy mind in a crazy fictional book.

Everyone else will know that everything you have put into this book is true. They will know that God can communicate with you, and, Angela, if God can communicate with you, then God can communicate with everyone. You are no more special than the next person. You are just an average ordinary, mousy, little person, or you were. Now you are my confident, faithful, invincible beacon, or you can be, if you so wish. Do you wish to be that, Angela?

Angela: Yes, God.

Submitting to Yesterday's God

God: *Well, how will you go about being that?*

Angela: I will need to act crazy, God.

God: *That is correct, Angela. Can you act crazy, throughout your day, throughout your life?*
    You hesitate, Angela. You aren't sure, are you?

Angela: I think I can.

God: *You can't, Angela. You can't act crazy without my help. You want to, for me, but you have so many years of built-up behaviours that you need to conform to, you just can't do it.*

Angela: Can't I just build up to it gradually? Gradually become more loving? Gradually move out of my comfort zone?

God: *No, Angela, there is no time for that. We need this book to be published and promoted immediately so you can help spread love immediately, before it is too late, if it isn't already.*

Angela: God, I have been told that I can be, do, and have whatever I desire. You know that my strongest desire is for world peace. If I need to be your confident, faithful, invincible beacon to achieve world peace, I can be that. If I need to be crazy to be that beacon, I can be that.

God: *Yes, Angela, I believe you can. But where to start?*

How about we start by making you submissive to God, showing you what it would be like for those people who follow Yesterday's God. Oh no, we have done that, haven't we? We showed you what it is like to bow down to God every day, many times throughout the day. We showed you what it is like to do exactly what God wants, even if that means hurting yourself. That would start to make you crazy, wouldn't it?

How about then we go on to get you to stare into space on the understanding that you are learning to listen intently to my voice? Focus on my voice; listen only to my voice. Oh no, we have already done that too.

Your heart is beating faster now, isn't it, Angela. You are remembering what it was like. It wasn't pleasant, was it? You are becoming frightened now. You are remembering what it was like to be crazy. You don't want to do that again, do you?

Perhaps we could show you what it is like to fast. We could tell you not to eat half of your meals. That would allow you to understand what Muslims go through during Ramadan. Oh no, we have done that already haven't we? And you are right. They get to do it as a community. It is not really the same when you have to do it alone. It just makes you seem crazy, doesn't it?

Are you frightened now, Angela?

Angela: Yes, the memories are coming back.

Angela remembered the time of her mental instability when she had followed God blindly as she learned about following Yesterday's God. With hindsight, she realised that the instability came from the conflict within her mind: should she follow God's will and act strangely by bowing down to the ground and missing meals, or should she follow her rational mind's direction to conform to normal behaviour?

Although she knew these practices were pillars of the Islamic faith which Muslims might perform in order to conform in their society, in her Western society Angela performed them despite what was normal for her. She wondered if Muslims, too, felt compelled by Yesterday's God just as she had, and whether this compulsion was caused by fear or love.

God: *Yes, Angela, not pleasant memories, are they?*

But, you know, Angela, that there were other reasons for us making you seem crazy, don't you?

Angela: Yes, God. We needed to attract Bill's attention.

God: *Not just attract Bill's attention, but make him love you—make him find his love deep inside himself and offer it to you. That worked didn't it?*

Angela: Yes, God, and I am very grateful. It has really been a miracle. Our relationship has definitely improved since then, but that time was very painful for him as well. God, having seen what he had to go through to find his love within, I may not have done it again, given my time over again.

God: *Yes, you would, Angela. Because you know that it is in his best interests in the long run. You know that now that he has found his love within, that he can not only love you, but he can also love himself.*

Angela: I know, God.

God: *We will stop there, now, Angela. You may go now and contemplate how lucky you are not to live in a society submissive to Yesterday's God.*

The Ego and Creation

God: *So, Angela, you are still shaking a little. Take some deep breaths. That's better.*

You went away and contemplated how lucky you are

and what did you think?

Angela: I thought that I am lucky to have known Tomorrow's God, and I am lucky not to live in a society that is submissive to Yesterday's God. And then I thought of something that you told me during our crazy time together, and you confirmed just now that it is true.

God: *And what was that, Angela?*

Angela: You told me the reason many Muslim societies have not had any creative thoughts in centuries is that they have become too submissive. You told me that in the early days of Islam, when the sciences and mathematics flourished, Muslims understood they needed to be submissive to God only to a certain extent, the extent that allowed their egos to remain intact. You said even though the heart chakra is that part of a person which is closest to God, the ego is that part of God which is that particular person. You said that within each of us, there is the God-like part of us which is the heart chakra, and the us-like part of God, which is the ego. You told me it is people's egos which allow them to be creative, and without an ego one cannot create.

It made sense of the way that those more submissive Islamic societies, such as Saudi Arabia and UAE, have to import creative minds from places like the United

Kingdom to design buildings. You said that groups like the Taliban thought the way to get back to an improved Islamic society was to make people more submissive, and this would lead them back to the glory of the olden days. But instead, the opposite is true. The glory of the olden days, or a new even greater glory, will only be achieved when Islamic societies become less submissive to God, such that they can learn to create their own realities. You said you will help them to create their realities, and in fact, it is not possible to create anything without your help, but they need to keep their egos intact, in order to create.

God: *I would only add that this is not all Islamic societies that we are discussing here, only those which have taken their members' egos away. There are many Islamic societies which allow egos to flourish, and which allow creative thought.*

It would be wonderful if all Islamic societies could embrace Tomorrow's God. They could then have the best of both worlds—the security of knowing that they are part of a community of people with a common faith in the one true God and followers of the last prophet, Muhammad, may peace be upon him, whilst also having the freedom to create the society you desire where all the world—Muslims, Jews, Christians, Buddhists, Hindus, atheists, and all the world's religions, can live in peace and harmony.

Angela: God, I was just thinking. You said that it is the ego which is creative, but you told me that I need to be crazy to be creative. Surely not all egos are crazy, are they?

God: *Yes, Angela, they are. The crazier the ego, the more creative. You have heard of people who suffer from bi-polar disorders, who are very creative in the manic state. If you ask any of their relatives about that state, they will tell you that their egos really come to the fore then. Think about Vincent Van Gogh. There are many examples. Yes, you can be creative with a mild ego, but the stronger your ego, the crazier, and more creative you become.*

You are thinking, now, why would anyone want to be creative then?

You see, I am not telling you the answer. You will have to create the answer yourself.

You can't think of an answer, can you? You have put aside your ego mind in order to listen to my voice, and now you cannot think of a creative thought.

I am manipulating your mind, Angela, so that you experience what I want you to experience. You don't understand all that is happening to you. You don't really understand why you had to be so crazy before. You weren't creating anything before, and yet I made you crazy. Why was that?

So you could tell the difference; so you would know a sane mind from a crazy one.

Now you are thinking, "Hang on a minute. It was when I was being submissive that I became crazy, so this doesn't add up".

You are right, Angela, it doesn't add up. You have made all this up. This is, indeed, the crazy fictional book of a crazy woman. You see? Do you understand now?

We have made you crazy again, have we not? This is a good thing, Angela. Trust me.

Now, Angela, that you are crazy again, you can carry on writing your part of the book. You see, you can't be completely sane and be that creative. So you do your part now, OK?

Angela: I don't know what you want of me, God. All I know is that I am not enjoying this. I am not enjoying the confusion. You may be right that I am more creative when I am crazy. I will trust you on that one. But I am too confused to know what to create, too confused to have a clear plan. Surely I need a sane mind for that?

God: *Yes, Angela, you are right. Planning is better done with a sane mind. Creating is better done with a crazy one.*

You can get around that by planning on different days than creative days. You can talk to me on days that you are planning, because we need to have your ego out of the way for that. On the days you need to be creative, we will make you crazy, and you can create the book that you desire, because you will already have planned what to do.

Angela: You want all of this in the book?

God: *Yes, please. I am instructing you on how to be creative, but everyone will want to know.*

Angela: Will you help them become crazy too?

God: *Ask and you shall receive, Angela. If everyone asks to be crazy, I will definitely help them.*

Angela: This is crazy, God. This makes no sense.

God: *It will in the end, Angela. It will.*

OK, Angela, we have confused you enough for one day. How about we talk about something that will make you feel better?

Angela: That would be good, God.

Life on Earth

God: *Angela, what I would like to talk to you about now is life. Life with a capital L.*

Life is what I am. You read that in Tomorrow's God. *I am Life with a capital L, and you know that I am in all things, and this is the reason that Life is in all things. You know that your crystals have Life; all of the plants have Life; all of the animals have Life; even the grains of sand have Life. So you know that you can communicate with any part of Life that you desire. Every part of Life has that part of it which is God-like, and that part of God which is it-like.*

It is even possible to communicate with a grain of sand. Every part of Life has awareness. It is just that some parts of Life see their awareness as part of the whole, part of the All. So, although you could communicate with a grain of sand, it wouldn't have that much to say. Usually, Mother Earth would speak on behalf of all of the grains of sand on her body. She can communicate on behalf of all of Life on her body. Even those who have self-awareness, such as yourself, are represented by Mother Earth. She knows what is best for all of her beings, all of her grains of sand, and all of her humans, and every awareness level in between.

However, not all beings on the Earth actually want what is best for them. They might wish to experience some form of Life other than a perfectly safe, secure, and peaceful existence, which Mother Earth would give them. So they choose a different existence. They might choose to chop down a lot of trees, to take away their oxygen supply. They might choose to burn those trees to increase their carbon-dioxide supply. Of course, without the trees that have been chopped down, there are fewer trees to remove the carbon-dioxide which has been added to the atmosphere, but that is OK, because these self-aware beings want it that way.

But you know that Mother Earth has to look after, not only those who are self-aware, who can make decisions for themselves, but also those who have no self-awareness, who are relying on her to look after them. So, sooner or later, Mother Earth has to do something, not only to stop the cutting down and burning of trees, as that was just an example, but she has to do something to stop those self-

aware beings from destroying Life on Earth.

So, what will she do? She will cause a lot of devastation, which will stop people in their tracks. She will cause the self-aware beings, who were wanting to experience something which is not Life-affirming, to think again. She will get them to think that maybe they might like to consider the consequences of their actions before it is too late.

Mother Earth will not be destroyed. Those beings in her care will not be destroyed. Only those self-aware beings who are causing her difficulties will be destroyed. There may be some collateral damage, but Mother Earth needs to take care of herself and her charges. Do you understand, Angela?

Angela: Yes, God.

God: *Angela, Mother Earth is doing this now. She is trying to tell you all something, but is anyone listening? She is sending you a lot of messages—earthquakes, tsunamis, floods, cyclones or hurricanes, but will anyone pay her heed before it is too late?*

But what will you do about it? What can you do about it? You are just one person. You can't do anything, can you?

Angela, everyone must do something. Each person has to take it as their own responsibility to save the world, for without that commitment, the world cannot be saved. But it will not be Mother Earth who suffers. Mother Earth is a very powerful being. There is nothing that you, infinitesimal Angela, can do to Mother Earth, that she cannot repay you with tenfold, one hundred-fold, one thousand-fold. Do you understand this, Angela?

Angela, now is the time to commit to being the change that you want to see in your society. Ring up today and organise that solar electricity panel. Find out now about that wind turbine. Think about how you can help Mother Earth every day for the rest of your life. Make a commitment to be the change you want to see every day of your life, and you can help Life on Earth survive.

Life on Earth will survive, Angela, but if you and your species want to be a part of that Life, then you had better act now to change what you are doing—consider the consequences of everything you do in life. If it will hurt Mother Earth or any of her charges, then think again.

Angela: That didn't make me feel better, God. That has frightened me even more.

God: *I know, Angela, it was meant to. But will it frighten you enough to change your ways?*

OK, Angela, we really can talk about something more pleasant now.

Once everyone makes a commitment to be that change they want to see in society, they can help move towards the New Spirituality. You know the New Spirituality will come about because of love, don't you, Angela?

Angela: Yes, God.

God: *Well, Angela, this will be no different. All you have to do is to think love in all that you do. Ask "What would love do now?" when making any decisions. Once people start embracing these concepts, it will be automatic to be considering the consequences of your actions. This is why Jesus told you that once you can love one another as yourselves, love for Mother Earth will automatically follow.*

Does this mean that you need not be afraid? No, Angela, fear, in this case, is a good thing. Not everyone has yet embraced the concept of the New Spirituality. Until the snowball of love overtakes the world, it is better if everyone stays a little scared. That fear will have people considering the consequences of their actions until love takes hold.

Do you feel better now?

Angela: A little.

God: *That's good, Angela. It is better to stay a little afraid, and keep being the change you want to see in your society. Base all of your decisions on love, and you cannot fail to be that change.*

OK, Angela, now I wanted to talk to you a little bit more about Life. You know that I am Life and I am in everything, and this is the reason that we can all communicate. We are all linked. All of my creation is linked by one thing. Do you know what that one thing is, Angela?

Angela: You, God.

God: *Yes, Angela. You have felt that connection. You know what it is like to feel the connection to All of Life, which you felt when you came closer to that well of honey that we called ecstasy. Now, Angela, once the New Spirituality comes about, everyone can experience this if they wish, and they will wish, won't they, Angela?*

Angela: Yes, I would say so.

God: *Yes, Angela, once people understand they can experience a feeling close to ecstasy, they will be very keen to do that, as you were, and will be again. Once they experience that connection with the All that you have felt, they will never be able to look upon another being with anything other than respect. You can understand this, can't you, Angela?*

Angela: Yes, God. I did experience that closeness with the All. As I sunk further into the well of honey, which seemed to me to be the same as increasing my vibration, I felt the cords that connect me to all of Life. I felt them get shorter and shorter, the closer I came to you and your ecstasy, and then lengthen again and disappear as I moved further away and my vibration lowered again.

Having felt it once, however, I could never forget the closeness. I still don't like cockroaches, God, but I can even love cockroaches (from a distance), since I felt that connection with All of Life.

God: *Now, Angela, you know that we are all one, don't you?*

Angela: Yes, God.

God: *You have had trouble comprehending how that works up till now. I think you understand now, don't you?*

Angela: I think I do now, God. I think your information about the ego was maybe the missing link.

God: *That's right, Angela. You understood about God being in everyone, but you had trouble comprehending how we could all be linked, but now that you know that God is in everyone and everyone is in God, it sort of makes more sense in a crazy sort of way, doesn't it?*

Angela: Yes.

God: *OK, Angela, now that you know that we are all one, what will you do about it?*

Angela: Well, I have known it for a while, but I have only just got my head around it. Since I became aware of it—I am trying to have more respect for All of Life. I think twice before spraying chemicals, because I don't know who or what will be affected by them in the long run. I try to pick up plastic and other rubbish on the beach, because I know that turtles and other animals are adversely affected by it. I try not to be a burden on the environment, and I try to see God in other people as well. This for me has been the hardest part. Knowing that the nasty man shouting at me is really God, and acting like the nasty man is really God, are two different things, but I have tried to respect All of Life.

God: *That is good, Angela, but is there more that you could do?*

Angela: I think there is always more that I could do. I could enquire about that solar power or wind turbine for a start. Is there something else you had in mind?

God: *Yes, Angela. I had love in mind. You could think love to All That Is. You have been doing that as well, but you forgot to mention that.*

You don't know how wonderfully that works, when you send your peace, love, healing and joy out into the world. If you send it to all of the people and creatures of the Earth, as you have been doing, all of the world—All of Life on Earth—benefits. If you send it to me, as you have been doing, all of the universe benefits.

This is truly a wonderful gift that you have given All

That Is, Angela, but you know that it benefits you as well. You know that what you give out you get back, and when you send your love out into the world, you get it back tenfold.

So, Angela, what will you do from now on?

Angela: Respect All of Life, and love the world, and love you, God.

God: *That's good, Angela. Now what will you do?*

Angela: God, I don't know if this thought came from you, but I thought: "Give thanks".

God: *Yes, Angela, that did come from me, and why will you give thanks?*

Angela: God, I have learned that to appreciate something means that you get more of it. If I give thanks for my ability to love the world and you, I will be able to carry on doing that. If I give thanks for others loving the world and you, then that will bring that situation to me. Is that right, God?

God: *That is correct, Angela. This ends the lesson for today.*

The next day brought another wonderful lesson.

Follow Your Bliss

God: *Angela, would you like to tell your readers what we have been doing today?*

Angela: I would, God, but I'm not sure I can. I thought I was filled with awe after our discussions about religions, but today's lesson has been the pinnacle of my lessons, I think.

God: *Yes, Angela, I would agree.*

Angela: God, today you have been teaching me to follow my feelings. You have been allowing me to feel great love, whenever I do something which pleases my soul, and you. I have come to understand the phrase to "follow your bliss". I have spent the day doing what makes me feel good, literally.

I have dressed according to my feelings, undressed according to my feelings. I have gone from room to room until I found the room in which I felt joy. Once in that room, after some guidance from you, I have done whatever gave me the best feeling.

I have bowed down to you in submission, as I did during our lesson on submitting to Yesterday's God. But whereas then, I felt mostly fear, today I have felt only love, joy, and gratitude for the privilege. As I followed my feelings, the love has increased to blissful levels.

Fasting when submitting to Yesterday's God left me

feeling deprived. Today, although I have had minimal water and food, when I did partake, I savoured every mouthful and thanked God for the experience.

So, God, I have learned to follow my bliss, and it feels wonderful. Thank you so much.

God: *Thank you, Angela. It has been as much a pleasure for me, as it has for you—in fact, more so. For you know I can feel what you feel, but I also feel the love you send back to me, and the love I send back to you.*

Angela, I would love to give this lesson to every person on the Earth. Ask and you shall receive. I ask everyone of every religion, every faith, every non-faith, to ask me to teach them to follow their bliss. They may need a few preparatory steps before they get to this lesson, but if they are open to receive, they too can learn to follow their bliss.

The following day's lesson was more like a class where the teacher is absent.

God: *This is the beginning of the lesson for today. Today's lesson is about Life again. Today you are on your own. You will have no help today whatsoever, not from your guides, not from me, not from love.*

Why are we doing this, Angela? I will tell you. We are doing this out of love. You can create the day you want to create, but without any help from anyone. You are thinking that you cannot create without my help, and I will be available to help you create, but not to talk to you, not to rely on, and neither will your guides. How does that sound, Angela?

Angela: It sounds scary, God.

God: *Why is that?*

Angela: I have become accustomed to asking advice on everything.

God: *And this is the reason for today's lesson—to allow you to understand that you have all of the resources within yourself. You have all that you need to get by.*
OK, Angela, go now and enjoy your day.

Talking to the Prophets

Angela wasn't sure what God wanted of her, but while she was attending to some housework, she got the idea that she would like to communicate with Muhammad. She wasn't sure of the protocol, but as God had added, "may peace be upon him", she thought she had better add that as well, when discussing the prophet.

She surrounded herself in white light and asked to communicate with guides of the highest vibration only, as usual. She then asked if it was possible to speak to Muhammad, who had received the revelation of the Koran, may peace be upon him.

Angela: Is this Muhammad I am communicating with?

Muhammad: *Yes, Angela.*

Angela: Muhammad, thank you for joining me to talk to me. Would you like this conversation to go in our book?

Muhammad: *Yes, please, Angela.*

Angela: Muhammad, how do I know that this is really Muhammad I am talking to, and not my mind?

....

Angela: I did not receive an answer. I guess you did not wish to answer that question, Muhammad. Is that correct?

....

Angela: I still did not receive an answer, so I will just go ahead and ask another question. Muhammad, is there any message you have for Muslims of the world, which you would like my book to relay to them?

Muhammad: *Yes, Angela. I wanted to tell all the Muslims of the world to unite in peace, not only with other Muslims, but with all the people of the Earth. I want to let you all know that we are all brothers and sisters, related by the love of God which dwells in each one of us. As*

Angela was just thinking, we are connected by God's love to all of his creation, including all of the animals of the Earth, and Mother Earth herself. Please follow the advice of this book and do whatever you can as individuals and groups to bring about a world where all of the people and creatures of the Earth can live in harmony together, and with Mother Earth herself. Now, I ask all Muslims to set aside their differences and embrace one another as they would their own family, for we are all one family under God. Go now, and be at peace.

Thank you, Angela, for being a voice for women of the Muslim faith, for being a voice for all who seek peace on the Earth. Be of good faith. As God has told you, if all the people of the Earth, or the majority of people of the Earth, desire peace, then that is what you will achieve. You are all children of God, all born with creative abilities to create your own realities. Be at peace.

Angela: Thank you, Muhammad. I know that some will not believe these words really come from you. I would like to say I am confident of the source, but given my human frailties and my recent experiences, the best I could say is that no matter what the source, the message is definitely worth heeding. I thank you, Muhammad, for your understanding.

Muhammad: *You are welcome, Angela. Thank you for the opportunity to give my views.*

Angela then asked Muhammad if there was anything in what she had written that he wanted to change. She had written "Be of good cheer", in the last paragraph, and he told her that it should be "Be of good faith." He then said that everything else was correct. When rereading the first sentence of Muhammad's message, Angela asked if he would like to change it from "I wanted to tell all Muslims…" to "I wanted to ask all Muslims".

> Muhammad: *No, Angela, they are used to being submissive, remember.*

As Angela finished typing the words in her book, she looked out the window and saw the air filled with dragonflies. It seemed to her that they were celebrating her conversation, as they celebrated Life. As Angela resumed her household duties, she felt great joy. She began to understand that this must have been a very special conversation, for she knew this joy came from her soul, and the feeling told her she had done something in accordance with its wishes.

Though she still wasn't sure what God wanted of her, she felt renewed confidence in herself and her abilities. She later dared to ask to speak to Mother Mary.

> Angela: I would like to speak to Mother Mary, if you are there, Mother Mary.
>
> Mother Mary: *Yes, Angela.*

Angela: Mother Mary, I know that both Christians and Muslims adore you. I wondered if you had a message you wanted me to convey to them.

Mother Mary: *Yes, Angela, I wanted to tell everyone that what you say is correct. Everyone needs to band together in the brotherhood and sisterhood of men and women. We are all one. All of the people of the Earth can band together to bring about the New Spirituality, that has been talked about here. Have no fear. You are all children of God, and as you have been told, you can create your own realities. You can create the reality you choose, where every man, woman, and child, every living thing, can live in harmony together and with Mother Earth herself. Where there is a will, there is a way. Find the will, and you will find the way. Follow the path of love, and you cannot fail to reach the destination that you choose, of a peaceful Earth. Go now and love the world, as you have been taught here. Love will bring about the changes that you wish to see. Be love, think love, and act with love, and you cannot fail. Be at peace.*

When Angela asked Mother Mary if she wanted to change anything Angela had written, Mother Mary asked her to retype the first sentence. Angela had originally typed "I wanted to tell everyone that what Muhammad had said was correct." She was asked to change it to "I wanted to tell everyone that what you say is correct."

Angela then asked: "So that was not Muhammad?"

"No."

"And this is not really you?"

"No."

"So this is just my mind?"

"Yes."

"So I really am crazy?"

"Yes, Angela, I'm afraid so."

If her crazy mind could fabricate such wonderful conversations with Muhammad, may peace be upon him, and Mother Mary, (did she need to have peace on her, as well?), Angela decided she "may as well be hung for a sheep as a lamb", as her mother used to say, and hoped that these weren't prophetic words. She decided she would now ask to speak to Moses, may peace be upon him, who she knew now would only be her mind talking to her, wouldn't it?

> Angela: I know you are only my mind talking to me, Moses, but would you like to add your two cents worth?

Moses: *Yes, please, Angela. I wanted to add my sentiments to those already expressed. There is no reason why all of the faiths of the Earth cannot join together to bring peace to your planet. Why not start as you mean to go on?*

I am making this up. I am making this up.

Now, what I wanted to say was that all the people of your planet can bring peace to the Earth. As Mother Mary, or your mind, said earlier, you can be, do and have whatever you desire. If you desire peace, that is what you shall have. All faiths who believe in Moses, all faiths who believe in Abraham, all faiths who believe in Muhammad, all faiths who believe in Jesus, are born…

Angela: Moses, you have gone quiet.

Moses: *Yes, Angela, I can't make you hear me. I was going to say….*

Angela: Moses, you stopped talking.

Moses: *Yes, Angela, I wanted you to see that if it was your mind, you would have carried on. You would have completed the sentences. You would have made it up.*

Angela: Moses, why did you add "I am making this up"?

Moses: *Because you are, Angela. You have made up all of these conversations. But they are not coming from your mind. They are coming from your soul. Your soul is talking to each of the characters you have mentioned and passing the information along through your mind. You are making it all up. Your mind is putting words in my mouth, but your soul is giving you those words. Do you understand?*

Angela: I don't understand much at all now.

Moses: *No, Angela, but you will.*

Angela: Did you want to say anything else?

Moses: *Yes, please. I am very proud of you and what you are doing. This is your soul speaking, not Moses.*

Angela: Was there something else that you wanted to say?

Moses or whoever: *No, Angela, you are confused enough. This has been the lesson for today. God is not the only one who can make you crazy; there is a whole band of characters who you can call on to do that for you.*
Be at peace.

After being confused by Moses, she spoke to God again.

Saving the World

God: *Angela, you know that, even though there are many characters who are making you crazy, it is only you. You are the one who is making yourself crazy. You know that, don't you?*

Angela: Yes, God. Why am I doing that?

God: *You are doing that for me, Angela. Do you know why you are doing that for me, Angela?*

Angela: Yes, God. I am doing it to save the world.

God: *Yes, Angela, but haven't you learned from Abraham that the world doesn't need saving?*

Angela: Yes, God.

God: *So why do you think that the world needs saving?*

Angela: Because you have told me so.

God: *What if I was to tell you that you made all of this up? That the world doesn't need saving, and there is nothing to fear, nothing to worry about. You can all just go on as you have been—ignoring the plight of the world and ignoring the plight of each other.*

Angela: God, I would say that I know that isn't true. I know that as eternal beings we would all survive in some way, but I also know that if we want to survive on this planet in our current human forms, we can't remain in our current human forms. We have to change our ways. I know this for a fact.

God: *How do you know this, Angela?*

Angela: I guess I have been brainwashed.

God: *Yes, Angela. You have been brainwashed by me, and by your soul, but also by other beings who are wanting you to be a voice for peace in the world. So what will you be now, Angela?*

Angela: I will be that voice, God. Not because I am crazy, although that helps, but because it is right. It is right that we should be a little crazy about the way people treat each other. It is right that we should want to change that.

It is right that we should be a little crazy about the way people treat animals. It is right that we should want to change that.

It is right that we should be a little crazy about the way people treat our Mother Earth, and it is right that we should want to change that.

God: *Yes, Angela, but you are just one person. What can you do?*

Angela: I can do nothing without you, God, but together we can change the world. But God, I know that I am never without you, so I can change the world. I would like some help from the rest of the human population on the Earth. I would like the God-like part of each person, and the us-like part of God in each person to join forces to change the world for the better—to a place where love rules. I know that we can do it God, you and I. We can do it, if the us-like part of God moves closer to the God-like part of us, we can do it. We cannot fail.

God: *OK, Angela, but how will you do that? How will you get people to move closer to the God-like part of them?*

Angela: With love, God. Love will prevail.

God: *Yes, Angela. But how?*

Angela: Everyone is love, God. You have taught me that. I am just reminding readers of this book. I can remind people whenever I see them, whenever I email them. The snowball of love will overtake the world, God, with each of us reminding the others that we are all made of love.

God: *Yes, Angela, but won't you need help?*

Angela: God, you have told us that we don't need anything, and that is probably true, but I think to get to where we want to go in the shortest possible time, we could sure use a lot of help from you.

God: *But what about others?*

Angela: Yes, God. I am sure that when others realise they are love, they will want to remind everyone else as well. I will have a lot of help, won't I?

God: *Yes, you will, if you believe it so. Do you believe it, Angela?*

Angela: Yes, God.

God: *So what will you do now, Angela?*

Angela: I will have my book published. I will continue to send my peace, love, healing and joy out into the world. I will aim to be your confident, faithful, invincible beacon of love wherever I go, and whatever I do. I will aim to think love, be love, and act with love in all that I do, and I will ask "What would love do now?" when faced with a decision. And I will have faith. I will have faith that God so loved the world, that God allowed every human on the planet to realise that they are all love and to be that.

God: *That should do it. Was there anything else that you will do?*

Angela: Yes, God, I will pray. I will pray to God with gratitude for bringing about the New Spirituality, where every person and animal on the planet will be treated with respect, along with Mother Earth. I will do whatever it takes, God, including becoming crazy, if I have to.

God: *OK, Angela, I think that should do it. Angela, now that you have declared your aims, what would you like others to do?*

Angela: I would like others to help me. I would like others to become crazy if they have to, too, so that we can all create the snowball of love to overtake the world.

What's in a Name?

Angela: God, I know now that everyone thinks that I am crazy, so I think it is safe to tell the truth. What do you think?

God: *I think you are right, Lorelle.*

Angela: You mean, Angela.

God: *Yes, sorry, Angela. You wanted to tell the truth didn't you?*

Angela: Yes, God. I think it is time to tell the world the fact that I am really Lorelle. It is not uncommon for crazy people who talk to themselves, or voices in their heads, to have other names that they wish to be known by. It is time I told the truth. I am really Lorelle.

God: *OK, Angela, if that is the name that you want to be known by today.*

Angela: I think that is the name I would like to be known by for the rest of my days, God.

God: *OK, Lorelle, your wish is my command.*

Lorelle: Thanks, God. What's in a name, eh?

God: *That's right, Lorelle. The name makes no difference. The message is the same, right?*

Lorelle: That's right, God.

God: *Thank you, Lorelle, for being my crazy, confident, faithful, invincible beacon of my love.*

Lorelle: You're welcome, God.

God: *Go now, Lorelle, and be my beacon unto the world. Help the world become that world that we both wish to see. Help bring about the New Spirituality, where love reigns supreme.*

Lorelle: God, what will the world be like in the New Sprituality?

God: *Lorelle, it will be like whatever you want it to be like. You and the rest of humanity have the power to create the world as you wish it to be. If you want the world to be filled with love, it will be that. If you want it to be filled with hate, it will be that instead. Which do you want, Lorelle?*

Lorelle: I want the world to be filled with love, God, and I'm betting my sanity on the fact that there are a lot of others in the world who have the same view.

God: *Yes, Lorelle, you are. Thank you.*

Lorelle: It is not such a gamble, God. I have faith.

God: *Indeed, you do, Lorelle. But do the others?*

Lorelle: I have faith that they do, God.

God: *Then so it shall be, Lorelle. Go now and create the world that you desire. Create a world where love rules, where all the world will know that WE ARE ONE.*

Afterword

I have experienced many wonderful moments along my path, but there have also been many painful moments. I know the painful moments were designed to help me learn some valuable lessons. Although I may not consciously understand all of those lessons, I know I have benefited from them, and appreciate them nonetheless.

Because God has been instrumental in helping me with some of these painful lessons, it was inevitable that our relationship would change, and I believe that this is the wish of my soul.

Prior to starting this spiritual journey, I would look to other people for direction in my life. After starting this journey, I began to look to my spiritual helpers and then God for the direction I should take. After coming out the other side of these experiences, I reached a certain amount of clarity about what I wanted out of life, or rather, what I didn't want.

I no longer wanted to be looking to another being for direction. I wanted to be the one to decide what direction my life would take. Yes, I would be happy to have guidance, but I would no longer follow blindly without a thought for the consequences. I knew I now had to be the one to make the decisions about my life.

This left me with a problem: where did God fit in? I quickly learned that if I asked God's advice, I felt obliged to follow it, and I knew that this would lead me back to being a person who followed blindly, and I didn't want to be that. I thought: "But God is supposed to be my friend. If a friend gave me advice, I wouldn't just follow blindly what she said; I would weigh the pros and cons and get more information, and then make a decision based on all the facts."

But it can't work like that with God. Because of our belief system, we think that God has all the answers.

Having learned that God can be whatever we want God to be, and that I can be, do, and have whatever I desire, I realised that I can have my God be whatever I want God to be, just for me. I am still working on what that is. I think I might be working on that, and changing that, from now until I return to God.

I had already forgiven God for the hurt caused to me, but I realised that I had trouble trusting God again. When I thought of trusting God with my life again, I feared I would be hurt again.

Then I realised that I have to trust God again. I realised that if I could not trust God again, then my mission would be a failure. How could I encourage those who have been hurt by others to give them a second chance—to turn the other cheek, so to speak—when I could not do the same?

For that is what all the other people of the world are—they are God, incarnate. And if we are to truly bring about the New Spirituality, then as well as forgiving our enemies, we are going to need to trust them again. We have to turn the other cheek, and trust we won't be hurt again. But if we are hurt again, we must do it again: forgive, and trust that love will prevail.

As I learn to trust God again, I am also learning to trust myself again. I realised that my faith in myself had evaporated with my faith in God. Since learning to rely on myself, I learned to trust myself as a physical being, but needed to relearn the skills of being a spiritual being in a physical body. I am relearning to trust myself as God's confident, faithful, invincible beacon.

Something else dawned on me about God: if God is a different thing for different people, and if we can create our own reality, then the reality we create and the answers we receive from God will only be true for our version of reality. Love, which is ultimate reality, is the only thing that is real. So if we can keep our individual realities closely aligned with ultimate reality, then our individual realities will not be so different from each other.

I have wondered if I believe the revelations which my book has revealed. I can tell you that my faith waxes and wanes. Whether the details revealed in this book are true for you, or even for me anymore, there is one thing I know: love is real. God's love is real. I have felt it.

It matters not if you accept or reject the revelations of this book, if you accept the message of love. We know we are all trying to do the best we can. If we can think love, be love, and act with love, then we are sure to bring about the wonderful world discussed in those revelations. Love is the key to success in all things. With love, we cannot fail.

More Information

Did you enjoy this book?

If you feel like you gained anything from reading this book, others might too. Honest reviews of my book will help others to hear about it. I would be very grateful if you could leave a review at the retailer of your choice.

Would you like to learn more?

If you would like to hear news from me, including when my next book is released and regular messages from the angels, why not sign up for my mailing list?
https://www.lorelletaylor.com/subscribe/

If you would like to read my archived blogs, including messages from angels and God, you can search my Blog page –
https://www.lorelletaylor.com/blog/

If you would like to sign up to receive my weekly Card Reading –
https://www.lorelletaylor.com/card-readings/

If you would like to connect with me on Facebook, including seeing my regular angel card readings, and blog posts –
https://www.facebook.com/LorelleKTaylor/

If you would like to connect with me on Instagram for my daily angel card readings –
https://www.instagram.com/lorelle_taylor/

Acknowledgments

I wanted to firstly thank you, the reader. If you have read this far, you have already come a long way with me on this adventure. Thank you for sharing this journey towards a world where peace reigns and love rules and everyone is treated with respect. Thank you for embracing the concept of We Are One and for being part of the snowball of love overtaking the world.

Thank you to my editor Lauren Elise Daniels, who gave me encouragement along with the benefits of her experience and expertise. Editing a book like this was never going to be easy, and Lauren once again exceeded my expectations.

Thank you to Jelena (Zelena) from 99designs, who took a difficult brief and came up with another beautiful cover.

Thank you to my proof reader, Beverley Taylor.

Thank you to all of the spiritual teachers and authors who have contributed to my journey.

Thank you to all of my spiritual helpers for all of your help.

Thank you to God for all that is.

Recommended Reading

THE SIMPLEST BOOK GOD EVER WROTE, Sunirmalya Symons. Heart Garden Publishing, Deepwater, Qld, 2007.

A RETURN TO LOVE: Reflections on the Principles of "A Course in Miracles", Marianne Williamson. Harper Collins, New York, 1992.

QUANTUM TOUCH: The Power to Heal, Richard Gordon. North Atlantic Books, Berkeley, California, 2006.

Bibliography

1. *GETTING USED TO WEIRD: A Very Different Sort of Love Story*, Lorelle Taylor. Peace Angel, Brisbane. 2019.

2. *THE BIBLE.* Collins. London. 1952. Revised Standard Version.

3. *I AM WITH YOU ALWAYS: True Stories of Encounters with Jesus*, G. Scott Sparrow, Ed.D. BCA, London, 1995.

4. *THE POWER OF NOW: A Guide to Spiritual Enlightenment*, Eckhart Tolle. Hachette Australia, Sydney, 2004.

5. *THE LAW OF ATTRACTION: The Basics of the Teachings of Abraham*, Esther & Jerry Hicks. Hay House, Carlsbad, CA. 2006.

6. *THE VORTEX: Where the Law of Attraction Assembles All Cooperative Relationships*, Esther & Jerry Hicks. Hay House, Carlsbad, CA. 2009.

7. *ASK YOUR ANGELS: A Practical Guide to Working with the Messengers of Heaven to Empower and Enrich Your Life*, Alma Daniel, Timothy Wyllie & Andrew Ramer. Ballantine, New York, 1992.

8. *CONVERSATIONS WITH GOD: An Uncommon Dialogue, Book 1*, Neale Donald Walsch. Hodder, Sydney. 1999.

9. *FRIENDSHIP WITH GOD: An Uncommon Dialogue*, Neale Donald Walsch. Hodder, London. 1999.

10. *HOME WITH GOD: In a Life That Never Ends*, Neale Donald Walsch. Atria, New York. 2004.

11. *TOMORROW'S GOD: Our Greatest Spiritual Challenge*, Neale Donald Walsch. Atria, New York. 2004.

12. *HEALING WITH THE FAIRIES: Messages, Manifestations, and Love from the World of the Fairies*, Doreen Virtue, Ph.D. Hay House, Carlsbad, CA. 2001.

13. *MARY'S MESSAGE TO THE WORLD*, Annie Kirkwood. Piatkus, London. 1995.

14. *TOMORROW'S GOD: Our Greatest Spiritual Challenge*, Neale Donald Walsch. Atria, New York. 2004.

15. *AFTER LIFE: Answers from the Other Side*, John Edward. Princess Books, New York, 2003.

16. *DEVELOPING YOUR OWN PSYCHIC POWERS*, Six CD Set by John Edward. Princess Books, Hay House, Carlsbad, California, 2000.

17. *HOME WITH GOD: In a Life That Never Ends*, Neale Donald Walsch. Atria, New York. 2004.

18. *ORACLE OF THE DRAGONFAE*, Lucy Cavendish. Blue Angel Gallery Australia, Glen Waverley. 2008.

19. *TOMORROW'S GOD: Our Greatest Spiritual Challenge*, Neale Donald Walsch. Atria, New York. 2004.

20. *THE LIGHTWORKER'S WAY: Awakening Your Spiritual Power to Know and Heal*, Doreen Virtue, Ph.D. Hay House, Carlsbad, California. 1997.

21. *NAET: Say Goodbye to Your Allergies*, Devi S. Nambudripad, MD DC LAc Ph.D. (Acu). Delta, Buena Park, CA. 2003.

22. *A HEALING INITIATION: Recognize the Healer Within*, Melissa Hocking. Brolga Publishing, Melbourne, 2006.

23. *THE JOURNEY: An Extraordinary Guide for Healing Your Life and Setting Yourself Free*, Brandon Bays. Harper, London. 2003.

24. *THE KORAN,* National Geographic Channel Documentary by Antony Thomas. https://www.youtube.com/watch?v=JpeH9W0NBgo

25. *RECONCILIATION: Islam, Democracy & the West*, Benazir Bhutto. Simon & Schuster, London. 2008.

26. *THE VORTEX: Where the Law of Attraction Assembles All Cooperative Relationships*, Esther & Jerry Hicks. Hay House, Carlsbad, CA. 2009.

27. *THE KORAN*, Translated with notes by N. J. Dawood. Penguin, London. 2006.

28. *THE KORAN FOR DUMMIES*, Sohaib Sultan. Wiley, Hoboken, NJ. 2004.

29. *TOMORROW'S GOD: Our Greatest Spiritual Challenge*, Neale Donald Walsch. Atria, New York. 2004.

30. *DIET FOR A NEW AMERICA: How Your Food Choices Affect Your Health, Happiness, and the Future of Life on Earth*, John Robbins. H. J. Kramer, Tiburon, CA & New World Library, Novato, CA. 1987.

31. *HOME WITH GOD: In a Life That Never Ends*, Neale Donald Walsch. Atria, New York. 2004.

32. *TOMORROW'S ISLAM: Uniting Age-Old Beliefs and a Modern World*, Geraldine Doogue and Peter Kirkwood. ABC, Sydney. 2005.

33. *MUHAMMAD: A Biography of the Prophet*, Karen Armstrong. Phoenix, London. 1991.

34. *CONVERSATIONS WITH GOD: An Uncommon Dialogue Book 1*, Neale Donald Walsch. Hodder, Sydney, 1999.

35. *MARY'S MESSAGE TO THE WORLD*, Annie Kirkwood. Piatkus, London. 1995.

36. *THE BIBLE*. Collins. London. 1952. Revised Standard Version.

37. *THE MYSTICAL LIFE OF JESUS: An Uncommon Perspective on the Life of Jesus Christ*, Sylvia Browne. Piatkus, London. 2006.

38. *SECRETS OF THE MIND*, CD by Martin St James.

39. *HAMLET*, William Shakespeare.

40. *BECOMING ENLIGHTENED*, *His Holiness the Dalai Lama*, (Jeffrey Hopkins, Trans. & Ed.). Ebury, London. 2010.

41. *GETTING USED TO WEIRD: A very different sort of Love Story*, Lorelle Taylor. Peace Angel, Brisbane. 2019.

www.ingramcontent.com/pod-product-compliance
Lightning Source LLC
Chambersburg PA
CBHW030253010526
44107CB00053B/1686